# Constance Mellor, M.C.S.P.

# Constance Mellor's Guide to Natural Health

*'Man is what he eats and drinks,*
*What he breathes, and what he thinks.'*

MAYFLOWER
**GRANADA PUBLISHING**
London Toronto Sydney New York

Published by Granada Publishing Limited
in Mayflower Books 1978
Reprinted 1979

ISBN 0 583 12783 5

First published by Health Science Press 1966
under the title *Handbook of Health*
Copyright © Constance Mellor, M.C.S.P. 1966

Granada Publishing Limited
Frogmore, St Albans, Herts AL2 2NF
and
3 Upper James Street, London W1R 4BP
1221 Avenue of the Americas, New York, NY 10020, USA
117 York Street, Sydney, NSW 2000, Australia
100 Skyway Avenue, Toronto, Ontario, Canada M9W 3A6
110 Northpark Centre, 2193 Johannesburg, South Africa
CML centre, Queen & Wyndham, Auckland 1, New Zealand

Made and printed in Great Britain by
Richard Clay (The Chaucer Press) Ltd
Bungay, Suffolk
Set in Linotype Times

Constance Mellor was born in Stoke-on-Trent. After she left school she became a full-time student at the Royal Academy of Music, studying singing and musical composition for three years. Her student years were followed by several years of public recitals and then by two and a half years of training to be a physiotherapist. After qualifying, she practised at various hospitals, and gradually built up a private practice in Hertfordshire where she has lived since 1934.

Since her retirement she has written another book – *Natural Remedies for Common Ailments* (also in Mayflower Books) – and numerous articles for health magazines.

Also by Constance Mellor

NATURAL REMEDIES FOR COMMON AILMENTS

# Contents

# FOREWORD

There is no single-factor formula for health.

Food, no matter how good, is not the complete answer. Other factors, such as pure air, pure water, sunshine, exercise, recreation, sleep, cleanliness (outer *and* inner), and wholesome mental and moral influences – all these factors are of the greatest importance in helping us to retain (or regain) good health.

Food, important as it is, is of value only in its physiological connections with all the other factors, each of which is indispensable to the needs and, therefore, to the health of the body.

After all, food is powerless, of itself, to build flesh, blood, bones, and nerves. Only a living, breathing organism can convert it into living tissues. Food is subordinate to life – to the Life-force inherent in every living creature. It is this mysterious Life-force that decides which and how much of the foods supplied to the body shall be built up into body-tissues.

It is, therefore, one thing to eat and drink the right body-building foods, but quite another to get the body to absorb and to utilize them. The body's power to do this depends upon the power of its innate Life-force. When this is at a low ebb, as in illness or when it has been sapped by excesses and other foolish expenditures, it is then futile to stuff the body with food – even the *right* kind – in the hope that this will cure the nervous exhaustion and build up the strength. It won't. What the body needs at such times is simply rest – nothing else. The power to digest and absorb food (lost, temporarily, through unwise expenditure of energy, or through illness) can be renewed and increased only by rest.

Just as the supply of a large pile of timber to a carpenter does not increase the productive capacity of that carpenter, so a large quantity of food, however good it may be, does not increase the digestive and assimilative capacity of the body. The living organism uses only what it *can* use of the foods given to it, the rest it discards. To eat, therefore, is not necessarily to absorb.

Nearly every day we see the truth of this statement. We see thin people eating lots of fattening foods without gaining an ounce in weight. We see invalids being fed with good nourishing foods and getting no better in consequence. We see anaemic people taking iron tonics and deriving no benefit from them. Indeed, the world is full of unfit people who have tried many diets, preparations, and special foods, and who have failed to derive benefit from any of them, partly because their digestive powers were feeble, but partly also because of their emotional and mental make up. Temperament plays havoc with the powers of the body to absorb and digest food properly, but it is something with which we are born, and unfortunately there is very little we can do about it, except to realize that it *does* influence bodily health to a tremendous extent. It is also the deciding factor in the *kind* of ailments from which we suffer.

In illness, the main aim should be to try and restore and to build up the body's powers of digestion and absorption by means of REST. This could (and sometimes does) include rest from solid food (see Chapter 12), for only rest of the whole organism can restore and conserve vital energy. (Digestion of food uses up a lot of energy.)

It is, therefore, as important to know when *not* to eat as to know what, and how much, to eat. Abstinence from food is wholly natural in illness – an occasional day of complete rest, including rest from solid food, is very beneficial to both body and mind. It is important, too, to sleep with your head to the north, so turn your bed so that its head and foot lie in a line running from magnetic north to south (or vice-versa). Sleeping in this position will help to recharge your inner batteries.

Following a day or two of complete rest on juices only, institute a feeding programme based on the lines which will be suggested in this book. Having read this programme, there will be no doubt in your mind as to which are the best foods to eat, but you may be a bit uncertain as to *how much* of each class of food you need. There should be no hard-and-fast rules about this, because everyone's individual needs are different, and what may be right amounts for you may be too little or too much for someone else. One person's capacity to absorb and to utilize the various food-ingredients is quite different from another's; consequently, you need different amounts for each. No one should feed according to arbitrary standards, based on the assumption that we all need the same daily amounts of each class of food. We don't, though usually our vitamin and mineral requirements are similar.

The amounts suggested in this book are based on the normal healthy requirements of the average individual, and are meant only as a general guide. Only you yourself can find out your own particular requirement of each class of food. This will vary according to what kind of work you do, what age you are, what size you are, what your energy output is and, above all, what your powers of digestion and absorption are. You need more than other people of the body-building foods (proteins) if you are a teenager, or a pregnant or nursing mother; even so, far more ill-health is caused by over-eating than by under-eating, and smaller amounts of the *right* foods are of greater value and are more easily absorbed than larger amounts of the wrong foods.

Usually, in illness, or when the body is debilitated, the body-cells are too weak to be able to extract the minerals brought to them by the bloodstream. This is when biochemic remedies are so valuable. Biochemic remedies are composed of minerals in a very finely ground state which are more easily assimilated by the cells than the coarser particles in food. (See *The Earth Heals Everything*, the story of Biochemistry, by Justice Glass, published by Peter Owen.) They supply the body's mineral deficiencies, and until these deficiencies are supplied, the body cannot get well. Or keep well.

## Chapter 1

# GOOD HEALTH – ITS BASIC PRINCIPLES

What *is* good health, and why is what we eat and drink so important to good health? Everyone knows the answer to the first part of the question. Good health is 100 per cent perfect functioning of every organ and tissue of the body, and this entails complete co-operation of body and mind.

Good health is the result of a clean slightly alkaline blood-stream, and this is conditional upon, and the result of:

1. *Eating less of the acid-producing foods than of the alkaline-producing.*
2. *Eating incompatible foods at different times, not together at the same meal.*
3. *Efficient elimination of wastes and toxic substances.*
4. *An absence of fear, worry, hate, and other harmful emotions.*

Apart from the bad effects of living unnatural, sedentary lives in fume-laden cities and of taking little or no exercise, health depends upon correct feeding, upon efficient elimination of waste products, and upon one's mental and emotional life.

Let us first deal with correct feeding.

It is no exaggeration to say that the vast majority of present-day people in the Western hemisphere are over-fed but under-nourished, chiefly because they lack a knowledge of a balanced diet and, as a consequence, feed on foodless foods.

To maintain good health is something no one can do *for* you. Your doctor can advise you about food (though he seldom does, except sometimes to tell you what *not* to eat) and he can give you medicines when you are ill (these usually suppress the symptoms without removing the cause of the trouble). But, if you want to feel 100 per cent fit, you have to make a personal effort – more effort than is entailed in getting a bottle of medicine from your doctor.

You have to take the trouble to find out (from books) the basic principles of body-chemistry which will indicate to you what substances the body needs (and *must* have) for its building and its maintenance.

Then you have to be painstaking enough to go out of your way to *find* the right substances (natural whole foods), and strong-minded enough to reject the wrong substances (the devitalized processed foods) simply because they are all too often easier to obtain and quicker to prepare. There is probably a health foods shop in your nearest town where the right foods *are* obtainable, but, if in doubt, send for a list of such shops to The National Association of Health Food Stores, 2 Brown Street, Stockport, Lancs. This association will, where possible, supply an address in countries abroad if the enquiry is accompanied by an International Reply Coupon (issued at a Post Office).

It is a public duty to keep as fit as possible so that (in the words of the song) we can – 'spread a little happiness' and so help others.

No one can do this who is not in good health. Our happiness, our success, our efficiency, and of course our life-span, all depend upon good health. This (our genetic constitution) we inherit to a very great extent from healthy parents and ancestors, but far more do we create it by right eating, right living, and right thinking.

Health can be sustained only by supplying the body with the right foods in the right amounts and combining them with due regard to their compatibility; by taking daily outdoor exercise; by getting sufficient sleep and relaxation of body *and* of mind; and last, but not least, by avoiding harmful mental and emotional states caused by worry, frustration, fear, hate, resentment, jealousy and so on.

There are two types of food:

1. *The alkaline-forming.*
2. *The acid-forming.*

Alkaline-forming foods include all vegetables, salads, tomatoes (uncooked), fruit, and milk.

Acid-forming foods include flesh foods, eggs, cheese, nuts (except almonds), cereals (except millet) and all forms of sugar (except honey).

In order to keep an alkaline balance of the blood, we should eat more of the alkaline-forming foods than of the acid-forming foods.

We should also learn to distinguish between compatible foods and incompatible foods, eating the latter at different meals. This is because, if they are eaten together, a toxic substance, known as histamine, is produced in the blood as the result of incomplete digestion of protein foods.

Histamine in the blood causes allergic complaints such as hay-fever, and asthma, migraine headaches, and general malaise.

The amount of histamine produced is considerably less when incompatible foods are eaten at different meals. Many people have found that, simply by avoiding wrong combinations of foods, they have lost their symptoms of ill-health, without recourse to any medical treatment whatsoever.

The following foods are incompatible when eaten together:

1. Protein foods with starches, sugars, and animal fats (butter, cream, etc.).
2. Starches and sugars with acid fruits (with sweet fruits such as dates, bananas, figs, raisins, sweet pears, etc., they are compatible).

Root vegetables do not get on too well with acid fruits. Milk, which is Nature's masterpiece, is compatible with most things, but is more beneficial if taken by itself. This is because, if it is taken with starch foods, most of its valuable calcium changes chemically, and becomes unavailable, *as calcium*, to the body.

Acid fruits are best eaten before a meal – never at the end – and only one kind at a time should be eaten. They are best eaten by themselves, not with other food (other than milk, or yoghourt).

By keeping an alkaline balance of the blood, you escape acidosis which produces rheumatism, duodenal ulcer, blood-pressure, kidney diseases, loss of appetite, lassitude, headaches, sleeplessness, etc. You also derive more benefit from the vitamins in your food, because vitamins can do their job better in an alkaline medium than in an acid one. This means that smaller amounts of them are needed and that these do you more good than larger amounts taken in an acid medium.

Most people look upon food as just something to please the palate and to fill them up inside. They don't give a thought to its purpose, nor to the miraculous way the digestive organs and their secretions break it up into its component elements, so that the body can absorb it and use it for heat, energy, and running repairs.

The body is the most wonderful chemical laboratory, but it cannot make good building-bricks (i.e. living bone cells, muscle cells, nerve cells, blood cells, etc.), without the right materials. It is important, therefore, to eat and drink the things that *do* contain the right materials.

It is true that 'a little of what you fancy does you good', but – don't eat what you fancy to the exclusion of things that you know are essential to good health. *Eat first what you should, then what you would*, Sir William Osler used to say! Having eaten what you should, you won't have much room left for what you *would*. This is all to the good, because present-day palates are not true guides to their owner's bodily needs. They have acquired a taste for refined sophisticated foods. These may look attractive, and (such is the cleverness of food-technologists) may taste attractive, but they are often unbalanced foodless foods which have been deprived of some, if not all, of their vital parts and are therefore no longer foods in the true sense of the word — such things as white flour and white sugar products (shop cakes, biscuits, jams, sweets, chocolates, white bread and rolls, etc.). These things have also had harmful substances *added to* them, to make them look and taste more attractive, and to give them a longer shelf life.

If, therefore, you truly seek health, start by re-educating your palate so that it learns to desire and to relish only natural whole foods. Do this by refraining from all food, other than fresh ripe fruit, for a day or two. You will then become so hungry that you will feel able to tackle a raw carrot. If you are really hungry, this, like other raw food, will taste very good.

There is, you see, a world of difference between real hunger and false hunger. The latter is appeased only by things that pander to the palate, and, if you give way to it, your desire for more important foods may never make itself felt. 'That sinking feeling' is very often due simply to fermentation in the stomach, and a few sips of water will usually dispel it. If it doesn't, eat an apple, some dates, or some raisins, not a bun and a cup of tea, neither of which contains any of the vital substances your body is crying out for.

The really vital and important foods are fresh ripe fruits, vegetables, and salads. These are 'live' foods — at least, they are until they are cooked — full of vitamins, minerals, and 'trace' elements (provided they have been grown on composted naturally fertilized soil, without artificial fertilizers).

They are full of stored sunlight, and sun-water (rain-water). What a pity it is to cook them, because cooking destroys their vitamins and digestive enzymes and extracts their minerals and trace elements; these dissolve in the cooking-water which, in the case of vegetables, is usually thrown away; it should, of course, be drunk as soup. (The addition of a little Vecon adds to its value and makes it taste delicious.)

It is wise, therefore, to get into the habit of eating as many things as possible in their natural raw state (beans are an exception; they are best eaten cooked). Remember that what is important is *not* the food in your life – but the life in your food.

The perfect answer to the problem of how to eat raw vegetables is a juice-press. This extracts the life-blood of the vegetables, which contains precious vitamins, and trace elements, without which our body-cells cannot make use of the other foods we eat.

Well-scrubbed unpeeled potatoes can be juiced, together with other vegetables.

If potatoes are cooked they should be cooked in their skins; this conserves their vital properties. Most health food shops can supply an electric juice-press, which might seem expensive, but it is an investment that pays big health dividends.

## Chapter 2

## HEALTH VIA FOOD

Our bodies are made up of what we put into them (food and drink), and all we can do about ill-health or disease, if and when it occurs, is to stop causing it. For we *do* cause it, chiefly by faulty feeding habits. Of course, our mental and emotional make-up (our temperament), which we inherit, is also an important factor in the cause of ill-health and in the type of ailments from which we suffer, but the major cause is a deficiency diet, combined with lack of exercise and fresh air.

'That's all very well, but what about illnesses caused by germs and viruses?' you may say.

The answer is, simply, that if a germ or virus *does* gain entry into a healthy bloodstream it will soon be destroyed and expelled from the body. The great thing, therefore, is to keep the blood healthy, free of toxic wastes and toxic substances, and slightly alkaline.

Even Louis Pasteur had to admit at the end of his life, that '*The soil is everything; the germ, nothing*' – by which he meant that germs cannot grow and multiply in a healthy bloodstream.

Negative emotions such as worry, fear, frustration and prolonged sadness upset normal body processes and cause acidity of the blood. If, at the same time, the body is incorrectly nourished with deficiency and acid-forming foods, the blood will become over-acid and overburdened with toxic wastes. On the other hand, if it is correctly nourished, blood-acidity will be kept down to a minimum.

Nothing curative can be done for illness that is due to purely physical causes except to correct the chemical background from which it springs. Every other curative effort is a meaningless and useless gesture which treats only symptoms and *not* underlying causes. These basic causes are:

1. *A bloodstream overloaded with acid and toxic wastes, the results of wrong feeding and of inefficient elimination of these toxic waste materials.*
2. *Undernourishment of the body, due to a deficiency diet.*

There is really no extraneous cause of disease – it is intrinsic to the body, created *by* the body itself, through faulty feeding. When deficiency-foods are eaten, the acid end-products of their digestion are produced in amounts greater than can be properly eliminated by the excretory organs. The consequence is that the body suffers from a retention of these acid end-products, and a toxic state of the blood becomes inevitable.

Sir Arbuthnot Lane, the well-known physician, confirmed this when he stated *'There is but one cause of disease – toxaemia, which means – poison. This is created through faulty eating and faulty elimination'*.

It follows, therefore, that any cure must be a self-cure – a nature-cure.

Nature has her own ways of repairing and curing bodily damage and disorder, and the only way in which you (*and* your doctor) can help Nature to cure you is by removing any obvious handicaps, such as toxic waste-products in the bloodstream (due to faulty feeding) and incomplete elimination of them.

Nature works slowly. It may be weeks, even months, before you begin to feel better as a result of your efforts to 'eat right, think right, and live right'.

However, gradually, as the blood becomes more alkaline through these efforts, the toxins that have accumulated in the body as a result of long years of wrong eating, wrong thinking, and wrong living will slowly be dissolved by the increasing alkalinity of the blood and will be carried away by it, to be expelled by the excretory organs – provided these organs are working efficiently (more about elimination later).

In illness, therefore – no matter what form the illness takes – aim at correcting blood-acidity by eating nothing but alkaline-forming foods for a few days (or even a few weeks) and, provided your mental and emotional processes are normal, your body tissues will restore themselves.

They will do so because the body is a self-curing, self-regulating organism, and recovery from illness is a function which only the body itself can perform. The self-curing power of the body is illustrated by the way in which a wound or a cut heals, and the way in which a broken bone knits together. The doctor can help only by setting the broken ends together correctly; he cannot make them knit together – only our body's inherent Life-force can do that. Symptoms of disease can, of course, be eased by medical and surgical treatment, but they will recur unless the underlying condition (the condition of the blood) is changed. (This statement does not refer to accidents and deformities, which are not *diseases*.)

The trouble is that, generally speaking, the medical profession treats symptoms rather than causes; it treats them with more and more harmful drugs (indeed, drugs are often the only things prescribed by doctors nowadays), or with surgical removal of what is really the result of an underlying toxaemia.

Such treatments may give temporary relief, but they can never cure because they do not remove the basic cause of the trouble, i.e., the toxic condition of the blood. Only by complete rest (and this should often include rest from solid food), combined with cleansing washes (external, *and* internal if necessary), followed by correct feeding, can the body be helped to cure itself.

If the blood is in an unhealthy acid condition due to emotional upset or to mental conflict and strain, the resulting illness is more difficult to cure than if it is caused by incorrect feeding or a deficiency diet (or both). Indeed, it will not be completely cured until the mind is again normal and calm. In the meantime, correct feeding – or *no* food, if there is no desire for food – will help to reduce blood-acidity to a minimum.

The body degenerates only as it becomes no longer able to cope with the rising tide of its own debris, i.e., with the acid 'end-products' of incorrect feeding and of mental or emotional conflicts. It can cope quite well with the normal day-by-day end-products of its own metabolism. These abnormal acid 'end-products' develop and accumulate in the blood as a result of eating not only the wrong foods but also of eating wrong combinations of even the *right* foods, because (as already explained in Chapter 1) some of these are incompatible with each other.

We should therefore learn not only to eat the right foods but to eat those of them that are incompatible at different mealtimes. To do this, we can continue to eat exactly the same foods (provided, of course, that they are natural 'whole' foods), combining them differently, that is all. This different combining involves simply a re-arrangement of the daily menus, so that no starches and sugars are eaten at the same time as proteins, and no acid fruits are eaten with starch and sugar foods.

If meals are planned with the idea of avoiding such incompatibles, the alkaline balance of the blood will be maintained, excess acid will not be produced, and body-weight will become normal, with a feeling of well-being and clearness of brain.

Thinness and obesity are both conditions which are the result of abnormal states of body-chemistry. These abnormal states are due to retention of the acid end-products of digestion which poison the blood, and the poisoned blood, flowing through the glands, upsets the delicate balance of the glandular secretions which control body-weight.

The brain, also, nourished by acid-laden blood, gets so befuddled that clear thinking is impeded. Memory, reasoning power, power to concentrate – all these suffer when the blood is overloaded with extra-normal acid 'end-products'.

Put this to the test by living for a day or two on fresh ripe fruits, and drinks of boiled water, and note the resulting clarity of brain. Not only will your brain be clearer, but your whole body will benefit. You will feel rejuvenated, years younger and pounds lighter, as if you had thrown off a heavy load – a load of debris – as, indeed, you have, provided your bowels have emptied themselves properly. To ensure that they do so and that your system has a thorough cleansing, take an early morning dose of 2 tea-spoonsful of Epsom salts in hot water before commencing the fast.

A short fast, combined with a bowel wash-out or an Epsom salts purge, is a cure for most minor (and some major) ailments. A longer fast, carried out under the supervision of a qualified naturopath, may be necessary for some major illnesses.

In normal health, the bowels can be kept in good working order by eating wholewheat bread, some 'roughage' in the form of fruits and vegetables, a spoonful or two of crude black molasses or black treacle, a cup of bran-tea sweetened with honey, and by avoiding white bread and white flour products, white sugar, and white sugar products.

Over-long retention of food-residue in the bowel (especially the residues of flesh foods) sets up putrefaction (a 'going-rotten' process), and this causes self-poisoning (toxaemia) unless bowel action is very efficient and takes place two or three times daily. Toxaemia can be reduced by eating less flesh foods (meat, fish, poultry, etc.), replacing them with cheese, milk, skim-milk powder, soya-bean flour, nuts and seeds of all kinds (including millet seed, sunflower seeds, sesame seed, etc.), eggs, lentils and lentil flour, pea flour, wheatgerm cereal, and brewer's yeast. Yoghourt discourages the growth of putrefactive bacteria in the bowel; so, too, does garlic. Both of them encourage the growth of beneficial bacteria.

Yoghourt is made of goat's milk and is obtainable from most health foods shops. It is rich in protein, and is very beneficial in the bowel. It is quite simple (and much cheaper) to make at home, of ordinary cow's milk (preferably farm-bottled unpasteurized).

To make it, write to Gilbert Harris, Fitzjohns Farm, Barby Road, Rugby (he is the maker of the goat's-milk yoghourt supplied to most health food shops), and he will send you the necessary 'culture' for making it, together with instructions. This will last for twenty-eight days, and will make as much as 4 pints of yoghourt a week.

## CHAPTER 3

# OUR DAILY NEEDS

When planning meals and menus there are four main things to remember:

1. *Every element the body needs must be included.*
2. *Incompatible foods should not be eaten together at the same meal.*
3. *As many foods as possible should be eaten in their natural (raw) state.*
4. *Worries and unpleasantnesses should not be carried to the table, because they decrease and inhibit the flow of digestive juices, and then the food, however excellent, and however deliciously prepared and cooked, stays partly undigested, its valuable nutrients are not absorbed and never reach the blood, and it simply passes through the body and is excreted.*

Every day the body needs:

*Protein*
*Natural carbohydrates*
*Fats (animal and vegetable)*
*Minerals, vitamins, and 'trace elements'*
*$1\frac{1}{2}$–2 pints water (amounts vary according to the weather and one's work).*

PROTEIN. Opinions vary as to the relative value of animal and vegetable protein. Let us not consider flesh foods as either necessary or healthful. On the contrary, consider them harmful, but milk, cheese, and eggs as necessary. These foods should constitute about three-quarters of our daily protein intake; the other quarter should be derived from nuts, seeds, pulses, whole-grains, brewer's yeast, and milk. About 25 per cent of our daily food total should be protein.

NATURAL CARBOHYDRATES. Under this heading can be included all fruits and vegetables, although usually only starch and sugar foods are spoken of as carbohydrates. If fruits and vegetables *are* included under this heading, then 50 per cent of our daily food should be carbohydrates.

FATS. Butter, cream, dripping, and lard are animal fats. Milk is rich in animal fat. Nut-butter, corn-oil margarine, soya-bean oil, wheatgerm oil, sunflower seed oil, olive oil, linseed oil, and almond oil are all vegetable fats. In cold weather one quarter of our total daily food-intake should be fats (half animal and half vegetable). In warm weather we need rather less.

MINERALS AND VITAMINS. Some of the minerals and vitamins required by the body are provided by the proteins, fats, and carbohydrates we eat.

For example, butter, eggs, and milk contain vitamin A and several minerals; wholewheat flour, wheatgerm, yeast, liver, and kidney, contain vitamin B; nuts, seeds and soya beans contain vitamin E; fish-liver oils contain vitamins A and D. However, most vitamins and minerals are provided by fresh fruits and vegetables, and the richest source of all-important 'trace elements' is kelp (dried seaweed).

Vegetables supply more alkaline minerals than do fruits; they are therefore better alkalinizers of the blood than fruits – especially citrus fruits, which contain a certain amount of free acid in addition to alkalis. Vegetables contain no acids. Another point in their favour is the fact that they contain more potassium, magnesium, and iron than fruits.

Of course, unless your fruits and vegetables are grown on rich organically fertilized soil, are ripe when picked, used as soon as picked, and eaten either raw or prepared without great loss of vitamins through improper cooking – you are probably not getting all the vitamins and minerals you need to keep you in good health.

It is a good idea, therefore, to grow all your own vegetables and fruits, as far as possible, so that you always eat fresh-picked garden produce, not stuff that is picked hours – sometimes days – before you get it. Fruit and vegetables quickly lose their vitamins after they are picked, so they should be eaten as soon as picked.

Our requirements are best supplied by certain foods because they supply a particular requirement in a concentrated form. For example, protein requirement is best supplied by lean meat, liver, kidney, fish, poultry, eggs, cheese, milk, skim-milk powder, buttermilk, yoghourt, nuts and seeds (especially millet seed), soya beans, soya-bean flour, lentils, etc.

Vegetable protein, supplemented by animal protein in the form of milk, yoghourt, cheese, and eggs, provides all the protein required by the body, and it is not necessary, therefore, to eat dead animals.

Vegetable protein is superior to flesh foods, for the following reasons:

1. *It contains potassium salts and thus helps to alkalinize the blood, whereas flesh foods contain sodium salts which tend to make the blood acid.*
2. *Vegetable protein does not cause putrefaction in the bowel; flesh foods do.*
3. *Vegetable protein contains no disease germs or viruses; the blood of animals (which of course is eaten with their flesh) often does. It also contains antibiotics and other drugs which have been given to the animal to fight the germs or viruses.*

Our protein requirements vary according to our age and to the size and weight of our body. An average-size man requires about 70 grams of protein a day; an average-size woman, about 65 grams – according to his or her normal weight. Pregnant and nursing mothers and growing children require 90–100 grams daily.

To get a rough guide to your protein requirements, measure your height, find out from a chart on a weighing-machine what weight you should be for your height, and, for every 2 lb. of this weight, a man needs 1 gram of protein daily, a woman slightly less.

For example, a man whose right weight for his height is eleven stone (i.e. 154 lb.) needs about 77 grams of protein daily; a woman of the same weight, about 70 grams. (*See list of protein foods and their comparative values, on page 31. Use it to check your protein intake.*)

Our protein requirement can and does vary from day to day, according to how we feel. Some days we don't feel we need much food of any kind, and it is wise on these days to eat only as much as we really desire – even none at all sometimes. The body keeps a reserve store of nourishment for such days as these (fasting days); indeed, it keeps a reserve store for several such days, and even for several weeks, if required. It cannot, however, store water, so this must be drunk every day. This need not be water from the tap; it can be the water contained in the juices of vegetables and fruits. This water is rainwater which is far purer and better to drink than tap water, to which a great many chemicals detrimental to health have been added.

Like all animals, our bodies are largely composed of protein, a lack of which results in low blood-pressure, lack of energy, anaemia, flabby muscles, obesity, poor digestion, low resistance to infections, etc.

Protein deficiency also causes a retention of waste fluids in the tissues, which give a deceptive plump appearance to the body. This is because there is a substance called albumin (made by our livers from protein) circulating in the blood-stream, which attracts fluids in the tissues and draws them back into the bloodstream.

In these fluids are dissolved the waste materials of the body's activities, and they are thus removed from the tissues and carried away in the bloodstream to the excretory organs (the bowels, the kidneys, the skin, and the lungs). Therefore we see that if the diet is so lacking in protein that the liver is unable to manufacture sufficient albumin, there will be insufficient albumin in the blood to attract the tissue fluids into the blood, and consequently tissue fluids (containing the waste materials) will not be collected (or only incompletely removed) and will cause an appearance of over-puffiness and plumpness.

People with such an appearance think merely that they are too fat, and they try to reduce their weight by cutting down their food intake (including protein). This still further reduces the amount of protein available for the manufacture of albumin, and their protein deficiency becomes severe.

Their body tissues become puffy, the ankles, face, and hands swell, puffy bags appear under their eyes, and the whole body becomes waterlogged. The chubby appearance of children, which is usually associated with health, *can* be due to retention of waste-products and water in the tissues. When a protein-rich diet is given to them, people soon lose their puffiness, and children lose their chubbiness and are then seen to be thin and underweight.

Protein enters into the composition of so many of the component parts of the body that its importance cannot be over-estimated. The part it plays in building bodily health should be better understood. It is the chief ingredient of the red blood cells, the white blood cells, the gamma-globulins produced by the liver (better known as 'anti-bodies'), the many different enzymes (digestive ferments), the hormones (chemical messengers) without all of which the body processes would come to a standstill. The afore-mentioned substance, albumin, is a protein-like substance which is also produced from food-protein (by the liver).

The white blood cells and the 'anti-bodies' are two of the defence mechanisms of the body which depend upon adequate protein, without which the body could not produce them. When protein is under-supplied to the body, the blood becomes deficient in white cells and anti-bodies, the defence mechanism of the body breaks down, and bacteria with their toxins gain entry into the bloodstream. It is now thought that the virus of poliomyelitis gains entry into the body in this way and for this reason, i.e. shortage of protein in the diet.

The white cells and the anti-bodies act as a militia guarding the health of the body. The white cells do it by surrounding the invading army of bacteria and eating them; the anti-bodies do it by combining with the invaders, putting them out of action, and rendering them harmless.

The average person thinks he gets enough protein if he eats, say, an egg for breakfast and a normal helping of meat, fish, or poultry at the main meal. But, if you refer to the Table of Food-values on page 31, you will see that those two items of food add up to only 22 grams of protein, and the normal daily requirement is more than double that amount.

It would seem to be essential, therefore, to include some extra form of protein in the daily diet. This protein could be any (or all) of the following: milk (preferably unpasteurized), yoghourt, cheese, nuts, seeds (sunflower seeds, sesame seeds, millet seeds), soya beans and soya-bean flour, lentils and lentil flour, skim-milk powder, wheatgerm, brewer's yeast powder, and casilan (this is milk-protein without the milk's fat and sugar).

Certain protein foods, such as meat, liver, kidneys, fish, poultry, cheese, eggs, soya beans, and milk, are spoken of as first-class proteins because they contain all the essential amino-acids (building blocks) needed by the body.

Other protein foods, such as lentils, peas, beans, cereals, seeds, and most nuts, are spoken of as second-class proteins because they lack one (or more) of the essential amino-acids needed by the body.

As we cannot ever be sure of getting *all* the amino-acids we need from second-class protein foods alone, no matter how much of them we eat, it is essential to eat some first-class protein every day, and to supplement it with some second-class protein, so that the total amount eaten by a man adds up to about 70 grams – by a woman, to about 60 grams.

But, because every first-class protein food contains *all*

the essential amino-acids, it is not necessary nor advisable to eat more than one first-class protein food at a meal. This does not mean that two different kinds of fish, or two different kinds of cheese (or of any other first-class protein) should not be eaten at the same meal. It simply means that two different *kinds* of first-class protein should not be eaten together.

For example, meat and fish are different *kinds* of first-class protein, so are meat and poultry. Meat and fish, therefore, should not both be eaten at the same meal; neither should meat and poultry (for the same reason).

If such combinations *are* eaten together at the same meal, the digestive organs are over-taxed; moreover, the body derives no extra benefit therefrom. However, second-class protein can, with benefit, be eaten at the same meal as first-class protein. Indeed, the two kinds enhance each other's value, a combination of the two kinds being of more dietetic value to the body than if they are eaten singly.

It is as well to remember, when reckoning up the amount of protein you expect to get from cereals and from seeds such as lentils, peas, beans, nuts, etc., that the protein-content of these crops is decreasing rapidly. This is due to the fact that our soil – indeed, the soil in all parts of the world – is wearing out faster than it can be rebuilt by present-day methods of agriculture, which use mostly artificial rather than organic fertilizers. Only organic methods of agriculture, i.e. putting back into the soil, in the form of compost, everything that came out of it, can produce protein-rich crops and, therefore, properly nourished animals and people. (See Chapter 15 – *Health and the Soil*.)

FATS furnish us with heat and energy. They are of two kinds – animal and vegetable. Both kinds are essential to the body, and a little of each should be eaten every day.

Animal fats (butter, cream, lard, and dripping) contain very little essential fatty acids (called E.F.A., for short). These are found chiefly in vegetable fats and vegetable oils (cold-pressed) and, as the name implies, are essential to the body.

Nuts and sunflower seeds are rich in vegetable fat; they also contain vitamin E, which is essential to many important body-processes.

Margarine is made with vegetable oils, but it is hardened by a process which destroys its E.F.A. content. It is therefore better to omit all fat when cooking. (Cake can be sliced and buttered when cold.) It is better also because, when subjected to heat treatment, all fats become indigestible and slightly toxic.

A spoonful of cold-pressed vegetable oil enhances the value and flavour of all vegetable or savoury dishes, and a spoonful mixed with an equal quantity of cider-vinegar, a dash of paprika and of kelp powder, makes an excellent salad dressing.

Insufficient vegetable fat or oil in the diet causes a shortage of E.F.A. in the blood, and this may eventually lead to hardening of the arteries (arteriosclerosis) and coronary thrombosis.

Keep all fats refrigerated, if possible, as even only slightly rancid fat kills vitamins in other foods we eat.

Keep butter in an airtight container and, like milk and cream, in a dark place. Milk left out on the step in full daylight loses much of its vitamin A content.

Vegetable fats and oils are better than animal fats for older people, though a little of each kind (vegetable and animal) is advisable.

Meat fat (which contains no E.F.A., no vitamins, and no minerals), is useless to the body. Without sufficient E.F.A. in the bloodstream, a vital substance called cholesterol, which is essential for cell building, accumulates on the walls of the blood vessels and furs them up – just as lime in hard water furs up the water pipes.

STARCHES AND SUGARS. These are fuel foods. A certain amount of fuel foods is necessary to produce heat and energy, especially in cold weather, but most people eat far too much of them – more than they need – leaving little or no room for the other important things, such as fruit and vegetables and salads.

The best fuel foods are wholewheat bread (preferably home-made), potatoes, bananas (tree-ripened, obtainable from some health foods shops, are best), honey, dates, raisins, cereals such as wheatgerm, barley-kernels, oatmeal, etc.

| Protein foods | Amount | Protein content in grams |
|---|---|---|
| Beef | About 3 oz. (an average helping) | 15 |
| Lamb chop | Medium size | 10 |
| Liver | About 3 oz. | 17 |
| Kidney | About 3 oz. | 11 |
| Chicken | Average helping | 16 |
| Milk (fresh) | 1 pint | 18 |
| Milk (dried) | 2 tablespoons | 7 |
| Yoghourt | ½-pint | 8 |
| Egg (new-laid) | One | 6 |
| Cheese (hard) | 2 oz. | 14 |
| Cream cheese | 1 tablespoon | 6 |
| Salmon | One third of a cup | 22 |
| Peanuts (shelled) | 1 oz. | 8 |
| Mixed nuts (shelled) | 1 oz. | Varies from 1–6 |
| Walnuts (shelled) | 1 oz. | 6 |
| Peanut flour | One cupful | 60 |
| Peanut butter | 1 tablespoon | 7 |
| Soya beans | Half a cup | 34 |
| Soya bean flour | Half a cup | 18 |
| Sunflower seeds | 1 oz. | 25 |
| Lentils | Half a cup | 9 |
| Dried peas | Half a cup | 12 |
| Dried peaflour | Half a cup | 12 |
| Wheatgerm cereal | Half a cup | 24 |
| Brewer's yeast (dried) | 1 tablespoon | 20 |

Preserves, also chocolate, made with brown Barbados sugar are obtainable from health foods shops. These are far superior to white-sugar products.

Flour-and-sugar products, such as cakes, biscuits, tarts,

puddings, pies, etc., are inferior in food value to bananas, dried fruits especially dates, and honey. Honey is the purest and best form of sugar (see Chapter 9). Glucose and saccharin are both synthetic substances and should never be eaten.

Use the list on page 31 to check your daily protein intake, remembering that most people need 60–70 grams daily, in the proportion of 50 per cent first-class protein and 50 per cent second-class.

## CHAPTER 4

## OUR DAILY NEEDS (MINERALS)

Minerals are as important to the body as vitamins; indeed, they can perform their functions only in association with vitamins (and vice-versa). When the diet is deficient in essential minerals the body cannot make use of the vitamins in foods, *no matter how much of them it gets*, and consequently it suffers a vitamin shortage as well as a mineral one.

There are about twenty mineral substances in the human body, of which nine are essential for vital bodily processes. As far as diet is concerned, four of these nine minerals are of great importance, and, by making provision in the daily diet for the ample supply of these four by eating foods grown in naturally fertilized soil, no serious deficiency of the others is likely to arise. The chief function of minerals is to keep the blood in an alkaline condition, although, as already stated, they also take part in vital bodily processes in close association with vitamins. The four important minerals are calcium, phosphorus, iron, and iodine (See Food Tables, page 114.)

CALCIUM

Chief sources are:

> *Cheese*
> *Raw milk (especially goats' milk)*
> *Cultured butter-milk, and yoghourt*
> *Dried skim-milk powder*

Minor sources are green leafy vegetables, lettuce and watercress, carrots, peas and beans (fresh *or* dried), almonds, black treacle, and black molasses. Cream contains little calcium.

The body requires at least one gram of calcium a day. It is particularly important for children and for pregnant and nursing mothers.

Its deficiency leads to improper building of bones and teeth, nervous excitability, and an inability to relax and to sleep properly; skin irritations; disturbance of the heart-beat and of the neutrality of the blood.

The British nation appears to be deficient in calcium. This apparent deficiency may be due not so much to a diet deficient in calcium-containing foods as to a lack of vitamin D in the diet, for the body is unable to utilize the calcium in foods if the diet is deficient in vitamin D (see page 43) This apparent calcium deficiency may also be due to eating to much animal fat which coats the lining of the intestines and so prevents calcium absorption through the intestinal lining.

Calcium, phosphorus and vitamin D are interdependent and work in close chemical combination with each other. They are essential each to the other. Calcium cannot be absorbed by the body unless the diet contains some vegetable fat and some vitamin D. Calcium in the form of bone-meal tablets should be taken with orange juice or lemonade. The acid of the fruit helps absorption.

Calcium is a wonderful remedy for pain of any kind – for headaches, period pains, migraine, pain of arthritis, muscle cramps, and even labour pains; also for nervous tension, irritability, insomnia, poor circulation and chilblains, and as a nerve sedative before ordeals.

During the week prior to menstruation, the blood-calcium sometimes falls to such an extent that nerviness and depression result. At the onset of menstruation, the blood-calcium may drop still further, causing menstrual cramps, which is really cramp of the muscular walls of the uterus. This condition usually occurs during adolescence when the demand for calcium in the growing body exceeds the supply, and it is then that calcium tablets in the form of bone-meal should be taken to supplement milk which is very often pasteurized and, therefore, deficient in calcium. Even if unpasteurized, it may not be taken in sufficient quantity to meet the calcium needs of the body. Milk is a complete food, ruined by pasteurization.

It is wise to take extra calcium during the year before menstruation begins, and again during the menopause. Women of all ages are more pleasant, and girls more manageable, if calcium is taken, because a sufficiency of calcium in the system soothes the nerves and avoids unpleasant symptoms such as hot flushes, mental depression, painful menstrual periods, and constipation due to a spastic bowel.

Calcium is essential for the proper assimilation of vitamin C, and is itself dependent upon the presence of vitamin D and of some vegetable fat in the diet, without which it is not absorbed by the body.

You may be getting an adequate amount of it and yet getting calcium-deficiency symptoms, simply because you are not assimilating it. An excessive amount of animal fat in the diet reduces calcium assimilation. Intake of sufficient calcium is one thing; getting the body to absorb it is quite another. The body *will* absorb it, but only if the diet includes enough vitamin D and excludes an excess of animal fats.

The richest sources of calcium are milk, powdered skim-milk, buttermilk, yoghourt, cheese, almonds, soya-bean flour, etc. (see page 114). The calcium and vitamin A content of milk varies with the cow, the pasture it feeds on, and the season of the year.

A pint of summer milk may contain 1 gram of calcium, but a pint of winter milk may contain as little as $\frac{1}{2}$ gram or even less. Dried skim-milk, which is made from summer milk when the pasture is green and lush, contains more calcium than liquid winter milk; so, in winter, it is a good idea to supplement your daily milk with a tablespoonful or two of dried skim-milk powder, and to eat a little more fat in the form of butter, vegetable oil, nuts, yoghourt and buttermilk.

Calcium-containing foods (milk, cheese, buttermilk and yoghourt) should, strictly speaking, never be eaten with starchy foods (bread, etc.). This is because if calcium reaches the intestines when starch digestion is going on there, little of it will be absorbed because it will combine chemically with the starchy food to form compounds that are not absorbable. Our calcium-containing foods, therefore, if we are relying upon them for our calcium supply, are best eaten alone, or else with protein.

The need of our tissues for calcium should be supplied by calcium in our diet. If this is deficient, the calcium stored in our bones is drawn upon in order to keep the calcium-content of the blood at a normal level; consequently, if the account at the calcium bank (in the bones) is overdrawn, our bones become brittle and porous, and our teeth rot quickly.

A jelly-like substance known as connective-tissue holds together the millions of cells of which the body is composed – rather like cement holds the bricks of a house together. Vitamin C enters into its formation, and calcium must be present before the jel will set. In other words, calcium is to the connective-tissue what pectin is to jam or jelly. Strong elastic connective-tissue is essential; it protects the body cells (whose walls are very thin) from harmful substances in the blood, such as poisons, toxins, drugs, viruses, etc. If there is a deficiency of vitamin C in the diet, the connective-tissue becomes so weak that, even though the supply of calcium is adequate, it cannot make use of it. Protection of the cells afforded by the connective-tissue is thus weakened, and invading noxious substances and germs gain entry. (See pages 42-3 for sources of vitamin C.)

Flesh foods contain much phosphorus. Meat eaters should, therefore, take extra calcium, to balance the extra phosphorus in meat; and the extra intake of calcium and phosphorus calls for extra vitamin D to deal with it.

## PHOSPHORUS

The body requires at least one and a half grams daily for much the same reasons as it requires one gram of calcium. (The two minerals work closely together.)

Foods richest in phosphorus are wheatgerm, milk, cheese, egg-yolk, walnuts, liver, sardines, herrings, halibut, tongue, brains, sweetbreads, brewer's yeast, sprouts, and runner beans.

It is an essential part of all the millions of cells of which the body is composed. Make sure of getting your daily supply by eating wholewheat bread from wholewheat flour from which the germ has not been extracted, and a new-laid egg. This also supplies vitamin D (provided the hen that laid it lives in the open air, exposed to light – not in a battery).

## IRON

Foods rich in iron are liver, egg-yolk, soya beans, lentils, wholewheat, black treacle, molasses, dates, raisins and grapes. Prunes, spinach and oatmeal are also rich in iron but should be eaten sparingly as, to some extent, they inhibit the absorption of calcium from other foods.

An adult requires at least 12 milligrams of iron daily. Adolescents require 15 milligrams (*see list of foods rich in iron and their comparative values on page 114. Use it to check your iron intake*).

The average daily diet in this country contains 5–10 milligrams of iron. It is apparent, therefore, that the average diet does not contain enough of the iron-rich foods to provide a sufficient amount of this most important mineral. Make sure of getting enough by taking one or two teaspoonsful of black molasses or black treacle in a glass of hot milk at bedtime, and by eating wholewheat bread. As with calcium, during pregnancy and adolescence the body requires even more than 12 milligrams a day.

To be able to absorb iron, the body must get an adequate supply of vitamin C, also traces of copper, from the diet.

Water from a copper-bottomed kettle will supply the traces of copper.

## IODINE

This is a trace element which stimulates glandular secretions. It is found in many vegetables, especially onions, cabbages, and celery. As with other minerals, it may be lost in the cooking-water, so the water in which vegetables are cooked should never be thrown away but should either be drunk or used as a basis for soup or sauce. Dairy-produce also contains iodine, but by far the richest source is anything that comes out of the sea, i.e. sea-fish, fish-liver oils, kelp (powdered seaweed) and Irish Moss (a sort of sea-plant). Powdered Irish Moss (Gelozone) should replace gelatine for making jellies. It is far more nutritious than gelatine, and very rich in iodine. It can also be used medicinally, for bronchial troubles, in the form of Irish Moss Zubes.

Iodine is a constituent of the thyroid gland whose activity is essential to the oxidation processes of the body. Iodine speeds up these processes, rather as bellows make the fire burn more brightly. Only a thousandth part of a milligram is needed by the body daily, but this minute quantity is essential, so make sure of getting it by using sea-salt or kelp (or both) in and on your food, instead of ordinary table-salt, which, like many other things nowadays, is chemically treated to make it smooth and white.

If you get symptoms of iodine-deficiency such as lack of energy and endurance, nervous tension, an inability to think clearly, or if you find you are an easy prey to germs going around, take (in addition to sea-salt or kelp with your food) one drop of medicinal iodine (it is called Lugol's Solution) in a little milk, about half an hour before a meal, twice a week, say on Tuesdays and Fridays.

## MINERALS FROM THE SEA

Nowadays most of our foods are grown in mineral-deficient soils. In addition, they are sprayed with poisonous insecticides so, not only do they fail to supply us with essential minerals, and vitamins, they contain injurious chemicals from sprays.

If we are to avoid mineral and vitamin deficiencies, therefore, we should add sea-plants and sea-salt to our diet. Sea-plants (seaweeds) contain all the known minerals (over fifty of them) and most of the known vitamins.

Among the minerals they contain are iodine (needed by the thyroid gland and by the brain), bromine (needed by the pituitary gland, iron (needed by the red blood-cells), calcium (needed by bone and nerve cells) and many others, some of which are entirely absent from land-grown foods.

As Dr Dudley Wright says in his wonderful book *Foods for Good Health and Healing*, published by Health Science Press, most marketed vegetables and fruits are deficient in many minerals and vitamins because the soil in which they are grown is depleted and impoverished.

Also the widespread use of chemical fertilizers tends to replace natural-soil minerals (in the structure of the plant) with unnatural chemicals, thus giving the plant an inorganic-mineral content rather than an organic-mineral content. For this reason thousands of people suffer chronic deficiencies which no amount of vegetables-and-fruit-eating can cure. These are the people who dose themselves with synthetic vitamin pills to replace the missing diet-essentials. They would do better to go to Nature's drug-store – the ocean – and get them in natural form from sea-plants which contain every mineral and every vitamin known.

Be it noted that *ocean water and the human blood are exactly similar in mineral composition*. This would seem to indicate that sea-plants constitute one of the most effective means of remineralizing the blood. They grow in the richest soil in the world (in sea-water). Therefore, in order to avoid mineral and trace-element shortage, the addition to the diet of sea-plants (seaweed, which is known as kelp) is an urgent necessity.

Kelp can be bought in powder form and can be sprinkled

over vegetables and salads, in place of table-salt which is a chemical compound, *not* a natural food. If not salty enough for your taste, a little sea-salt can be added – this is a natural product – almost (but not quite) as good as kelp.

Most of the table-salt eaten at a meal passes out of the body via the kidneys and bladder, soon after the meal, clearly showing that the body cannot use, and does not want, salt in this form – (sodium chloride). The body expels it, as it would an injurious foreign body. In passing through the kidneys, table-salt is apt to injure these organs; indeed, kidney injury is inevitable if the salt-eating habit is continued for a sufficient length of time.

In heart and kidney conditions and in cancer, table-salt is prohibited by specialists who understand its harmful action. It is strongly condemned by Dr Maud Fere in her book *Cancer, its Dietetic Cause and Cure*, published by Gateway Book Co.

## CHAPTER 5

## OUR DAILY NEEDS
## (VITAMINS AND TRACE ELEMENTS)

All vitamins are of great importance to the body. They work in close co-operation with minerals, which are necessary to the success of their work (and vice versa). During pregnancy and lactation larger amounts of both are needed; nursing mothers would enhance the value of their milk if they took one teaspoonful of cod (or halibut) liver oil a day.

VITAMIN A. Fish-liver oils are the richest sources of vitamin A. It is also found in carrots, liver, kidneys, butter, cream, milk, spinach, watercress, tomatoes, and sun-dried apricots. It is destroyed by exposure to air and to light, hence the necessity for keeping butter in a covered container, and milk and cream in the dark.

The vitamin A content of dairy-produce depends upon the amount of vitamin A in the cow's food, and so dairy produce is richer in vitamin A in the summer, when fresh grass is eaten by the cow, than in the winter, when dried grass is available. The vitamin A in carrots is in the red colouring-matter called carotin.

A deficiency of vitamin A results in dry skin, night-blindness, and a lowered resistance to infection. Adults need more of it than children. One halibut-liver oil capsule a day, together with the A vitamin in the above foods (some of which we should eat every day), supplies all the A and the D vitamins that we require (see Food-Tables, page 114).

VITAMIN B. There are about twenty members of the B group of vitamins, twelve of which are important; but, generally speaking, if your diet contains vitamins B1, 2, and 3, it will include the other nine. Brewer's yeast contains all the B vitamins except B12, but this can be obtained from liver (or dried liver tablets), from eggs, yoghourt, soya-beans, peanuts, and comfrey herb tea.

B vitamins are also self-manufactured, by bacteria in our intestines, especially if yoghourt, which encourages their growth, is eaten. A shortage of vitamin B 12 is very often the cause of retarded growth and of gawkiness in teenagers.

VITAMIN B1. You need this vitamin for the complete digestion of starches and sugars, for strong nerves and heart, and for energy. It is found chiefly in the growing centre of grains, e.g. in the germ of wheat. It is found also in brewer's yeast, wholewheat flour, millet, milk, and yoghourt.

VITAMIN B2. Very important for healthy skin, good eye-sight, and for obtaining energy from our starches and sugars. Best sources are liver and brewer's yeast, but, if these foods are not eaten every day, milk should be taken to replace them. Green vegetables also supply this vitamin.

VITAMIN B3. This also is necessary for the proper diges-tion of starches and sugars. Best sources are brewer's yeast, liver, wheatgerm, nuts, and eggs. A lack of vitamin B3 results in nervous tension, insomnia, irritability, sore red tongue, rough red skin. You get an adequate supply of all the B vitamins if you eat wholewheat bread, wheatgerm cereal, liver (or dried liver tablets), fish roe, potatoes, tomatoes, carrots, skim-milk powder, nuts, Marmite, and brewer's yeast.

VITAMIN C. A lack of this vitamin results in brittle walls of blood vessels, brittle bones, painful joints, easy bruising, unhealthy teeth and bleeding gums, duodenal ulcers, frequent colds through lowered resistance to 'cold' germs, susceptibility to other germs, and many other disorders. A lack of vitamin C is also thought to be a contributory cause of cancer. Richest sources of vitamin C are blackcurrants, rose-hips, oranges, lemons, tomatoes, carrots, swedes, cabbage, sprouts, English walnuts, fish roe, etc. Vitamin C in tablet form (made of dried rose-hips) will keep colds (and other infections) at bay. If you feel a cold coming on, take one 100 milligram tablet every hour until the symptoms disappear. You cannot overdose yourself with vitamin C. The body excretes what it does not need.

VITAMIN D. Without this vitamin the body cannot absorb calcium from foods such as milk and cheese, and poor bones and teeth are the result, also poor circulation and chilblains. Vitamin D is relatively scanty in foods. The chief sources are fish-liver oils, herrings, liver, kidneys, butter, yolk of egg, and bananas. The body is endowed with the capacity to manufacture vitamin D. This is accomplished by exposure of the body to the ultra-violet rays of the sun which act upon an oily substance in the skin (provided it hasn't all been washed away by too much soap and water) to form vitamin D; but, unless done very gradually, exposure of the body to the sun is dangerous.

In the winter, when we are not able to sun-bathe we do not, of course, manufacture any vitamin D, so then it is wise to take one halibut-liver oil capsule a day. This contains 500 mgs of vitamin D, and about 5,000 mgs of vitamin A.

VITAMIN E. The most important function of vitamin E is to prevent the destruction of vitamin A. Vitamin E is the 'energy' vitamin, closely concerned in the efficiency of the reproductive system. Deficiency of it results in sterility. The best sources are seeds and nuts, wheatgerm, and soya-bean oil. Minor sources are eggs, milk, lettuce, watercress and royal jelly (this is produced by bees for their queen).

VITAMIN K. This vitamin (also calcium), enables the blood to clot properly; otherwise, when you are cut or undergo surgical treatment, if you are deficient in vitamin K, your blood will not clot. It is one of the vitamins which the body can make itself (a little of it is made by intestinal bacteria).

The chief source of supply is milk, soya-bean oil, nuts, tomatoes, green vegetables (especially carrot tops), and peanuts. Intestinal bacteria, which produce it, can be encouraged to multiply by eating yoghourt and butter-milk.

VITAMIN P. You need this for healthy veins and arteries, prevention of strokes, etc. Best sources are lemons and oranges, especially the peel. This can be soaked in water overnight, and the water drunk, though it is not advised in these days when poisonous sprays are used on fruit. Vitamins are manufactured in small amounts by our intestinal bacteria, the amounts produced depending on the state of our intestines; e.g. if drugs such as antibiotics have been taken they destroy the intestinal bacteria which manufacture the vitamins, so these drugs not only kill the harmful bacteria, they kill the beneficial ones also.

All freshly-gathered fruit, vegetables, grains, and nuts, contain vitamins as well as minerals, so that, if we include them in our daily diet (preferably eaten raw), we need fear no vitamin or mineral shortage.

The amount of vitamins and minerals in them depends, of course, entirely upon the soil in which they have been grown; artificial fertilizers are not nearly so productive of 'quality' foods as natural organic fertilizers such as compost and manure.

Unfortunately most present-day commercial growers use artificial fertilizers because they are easier to get and quicker to use than natural compost and manure. They produce quantity and size, but the products fed with them lack taste and quality – this is because they lack vitamins, minerals, and trace elements. Commercial growers also use poisonous sprays, insecticides, and weed-killers on growing crops. These are harmful to the soil *and* to the people who eat the crops.

It is, however, possible to obtain compost-grown, unsprayed fruit, vegetables, and cereals. Some health foods shops stock them. If you don't live in or near London, you may be able to find a local grower who would supply you, but why not be independent and grow them yourself?

If you have no garden you cannot do so, but if you have even a few square yards of soil or lawn, you would be wise to turn it into a vegetable plot and grow just enough of everything for your own use, fertilizing it with home-made compost, bone-meal, 'Maxicrop' (seaweed) and rainwater (this is much better than tap water).

You would then have fruit and vegetables, free from harmful chemicals, that have been grown in rich soil and are full of vitamins and all the essential minerals and trace elements; moreover, they would be fresh and still alive when you get them. Vegetables from shops are nearly always a day old (or more) when you get them, and, in consequence, have lost much of their vitamin content.

It is a pity to kill the vitamins and enzymes in vegetables by cooking them.

Why not invest in a juice-press?

It lasts a lifetime, and the benefit your health would derive from the use of it would be worth a good deal more to you than the price you pay for it. Raw vegetable juices, extracted from vegetables grown on naturally fertilized soil, are invaluable to health, and are the best food *and* medicine in illness. Also make your own bread and cakes, so that you can get the benefit of the vitamins, minerals, etc. in wholewheat flour made from English wholewheat grain, grown on composted land.

Such flour is obtainable at health foods shops everywhere – in some towns, it can be obtained from local grocers. Use only brown (Barbados) sugar instead of white denatured sugar (which has been so refined that it has lost all its vitamins and minerals), and supplement with honey, molasses, and black treacle. Also, make your own marmalade, using Barbados sugar. This 'sets' just as well as white sugar.

## TRACE ELEMENTS

The body, which works on the minimum of anything it requires, needs only minute quantities (or traces) of certain other elements, which, for that reason, are called 'trace' elements. The richest source of all trace elements is sea-weed – its other name is kelp.

One of the most important trace elements is *iodine*, with which I dealt on page 38. It is required by the thyroid gland for its efficient functioning. Harmful germs are killed as they pass in the blood through the gland, one of whose functions is to deal with such germs. So we see that, in this way, iodine is related to the body's ability to resist disease. It is also related to the amount of energy and endurance the body possesses, and it's the match that starts the fire that burns up our daily food to make energy and heat. If not properly burned up, food is stored as fat.

Another function of iodine is to help the brain to work better. Clear thinking is impossible without a trace of iodine in the blood. Still another function of iodine is to calm the body and relieve nervous tension, irritability, and insomnia.

Iodine is extracted from the blood by the thyroid gland which stores it. If we drink water to which chlorine or sodium-fluoride has been added – or if we eat too much sodium-chloride (common salt) – the thyroid gland may be made to lose its stored iodine. This is because iodine, which has a heavier 'atomic' weight than sodium-fluoride and chlorine, is displaced (as are other substances) by things whose atomic weight is lighter.

You can eliminate chlorine from water by boiling it, but there is nothing much you can do about sodium-fluoride, except move to a district where the water is not fluoridated, or buy a distilling plant, or drink only filtered rain or spring water.

You can step-up the iodine content of your blood as follows:

1. *By eating foods rich in iodine. These are: sea-fish, sea-weed (it is called kelp), carrots, potatoes, peas, spinach, cabbage, onions, tomatoes, lettuce, bananas, and egg-yolk.*
2. *By taking 1 drop (or 2 drops if you weigh more than*

*150 lb) of Lugol's Solution, twice a week; this is medicinal iodine, and it can be purchased at any chemist's shop, together with a small glass dropper for measuring the dose exactly. It is best taken in vegetable juices about 15 minutes before the main meal.*

Unless there is an epidemic of colds or 'flu or other infectious things going around, the iodine need not be taken more than twice a week.

3. *By using kelp-powder instead of table-salt, on salads and vegetables. Kelp is the perfect answer to the problem of how to obtain all the 'trace elements' we need for health. The soil in which our foods are grown is being depleted of these all-important elements and minerals by floods, heavy rains, and bad farming methods; they get washed away and carried into the seas and oceans where they get absorbed by sea-weeds and other sea-plants. Thus the sea becomes the richest soil (in minerals and trace elements) in the world.*

Another very important trace element is *potassium*.

This is lacking in the soil of Great Britain which is an old country (it has been used up). It is thought by some eminent authorities that one of the causes of the modern tendency to cancerous growths is a shortage of potassium in the body, due, no doubt, to a shortage of potassium in the soil on which our food is grown. Let us hope that man will some day learn that soil-health, plant-health, animal-health, and human-health are all interdependent – that if the soil is sick (i.e. starved of minerals) there is a break in the cycle, and they will all suffer in consequence.

To cure soil sickness, all we need to do is to add organic compounds to the soil – Nature will do the rest.

Inorganic compounds (out of a bag) are no good – the perennial rhythm of Nature is interrupted by adding such minerals to the soil. Only by returning to the soil, in the form of compost, what has been taken out of it will soil starvation and soil sickness be cured, and, until it *is* cured, plant, animal, and human starvation and sickness will continue.

Sodium chloride (common salt) robs the body of potassium, and, as the body needs twice as much potassium as sodium, especially as one grows older, it is wise to omit salt and salty foods from the diet and to use kelp powder, celery powder, paprika-pepper, and sea-salt (which is a balanced mixture of many minerals) instead. Avoid fluoridated drinking-water; it destroys potassium.

Other foods rich in potassium are:

*Apples and apple-juice; cider-vinegar; grapes and grape-juice; honey; crude black molasses; fruit and berries; green vegetables (especially nettles); watercress; dandelion leaves, and tomatoes.*

A lack of potassium can be a contributory cause of arthritis, constipation, high blood-pressure, muscle-cramps, muscle twitchings, sleeplessness, an inability to relax, pimples, itching of the skin, loss of appetite, colds, cold hands and feet, mental and muscle fatigue, mental sluggishness, and cancer.

MAGNESIUM is a component of chlorophyll and, as chlorophyll is found in all green leafy vegetables, it follows that green leafy vegetables, especially nettles, are the richest source of magnesium, which is an important trace element. People who lack it in their blood are nervy and irritable; indeed, it is thought that a lack of it may cause a tendency to insanity.

MANGANESE is a trace element whose exact function in the body is not fully understood. It seems to be connected with the normal functioning of the reproductive organs. Like the other trace elements, it is needed by the body only in minute amounts but these are absolutely essential.

Potassium, magnesium, and manganese deficiencies in the body can be due to a lack of these elements in the soil on which our foods are grown, or to eating over-refined foods such as white flour, white sugar, etc., or to throwing away instead of drinking the water in which vegetables have been boiled.

(*The above remark applies, of course, not only to these three trace elements but to all minerals and trace elements.*)

SODIUM AND CHLORINE are trace elements found in so many foods that there is little risk of a deficiency of them in the body under normal conditions. Abnormal conditions, such as very hot weather, or living in very hot climates, or working in very hot places such as boiler-rooms, furnaces, etc., call for extra sodium because so much is lost in perspiration. It is best taken in the form of sea-salt (purified for the table by Tidmans).

COBALT, a shortage of which can cause pernicious anaemia, is a trace element which forms part of vitamin B12. It is found in liver, dried liver, peanuts, and 'Velactin' (a plant-milk made from soya-beans).

COPPER is another important trace element, a shortage of which can cause anaemia. The use of copper cooking vessels or a copper kettle will help to rectify the shortage, but wholewheat bread and Barbados sugar should be eaten because they contain it.

ALUMINIUM. This trace element is found in many foods, so if we use aluminium vessels for cooking we are likely to get an overdose of it. It is very soluble, especially in acids; therefore, never cook acid fruit in an aluminium saucepan – it is, indeed, safer never to cook anything in aluminium vessels.

## CHAPTER 6

## THE NEED FOR SUPPLEMENTS

It is an indisputable fact that proper nutrition is the basis of good health. It is equally true that *every disease known to man, from defective teeth to cancer*, is due to improper food, food that causes disease principally because of its lack of the essential elements that the body must have, or die. Even proper food (properly grown on fertile soil) is nowadays turned into improper adulterated food, unsafe for human consumption, by the addition to it of hundreds of chemical substances. It is also over-refined, denatured, and robbed of its vitamins and minerals by processing and other unnatural treatments and refinements.

Our forefathers, with no knowledge of vitamins, minerals and the like, were able to maintain a high degree of health on an ordinary simple diet, because their foods were not tampered with, not refined, not processed, and because their cereals, vegetables, fruits, etc., were grown in naturally fertilized soil. (Artificial fertilizers were unknown and not needed, because everything that came out of the earth was put back into it in the form of compost and animal wastes.)

As a consquence, their healthy crops contained all the vital elements their bodies needed for the maintenance of good health. Their meat, milk, and eggs, also contained more of these elements than ours do, because their animals' foods were more nutritious than present-day animal fodder, and were uncontaminated by modern poison sprays and insecticides. Also, our forefathers were ignorant of how to refine their cereals, and they ate, therefore, bread made of grain that had not been deprived of its vital parts (its germ and its bran). For sweetening they had only honey from their own bees.

Each family usually grew its own vegetables and fruits, often its own cereals too, and produced its own milk and eggs, if not its own meat – for, in the good old days, England was an agricultural country – consequently, most people spent a lot of time out of doors, growing their own food and their animals' fodder, and the fresh air and the exercise, as essential for health as the right foods, helped to make them into fine strong men and women.

These sturdy forefathers had little soap, and no water-heaters, so they were not able to wash off all the natural oils from the surface of their skins, and so prevent the formation of vitamin D when exposed to summer sunlight.

Unlike them, we, today, have lots of soap and hot water, which are, of course, a great comfort and help, but we tend to over-use them, especially soap. They remove the natural oils on the skin, with which ultra-violet rays in sunlight combine to form vitamin D, thus depriving us of this self-made form of the vitamin. This means that we must get our supply of vitamin D from the foods we eat, and this isn't easy because not many foods contain vitamin D in appreciable amounts, except fish-liver oils (cod-liver oil and halibut-liver oil).

Of course, if such wholesome fare were still available, supplements would rarely be needed (except for vitamin D, the sunshine vitamin) but nowadays it is not everyone who can obtain wholesome foods, yet they *can* be obtained from health food shops.

By wholesome is meant fruits, vegetables and grains, grown on naturally composted soil, untouched by 'smog', chemical fertilizers, and poisoned sprays; milk from healthy animals grazed in green fields; eggs laid by hens allowed to run about in the sun and air, i.e., fertile eggs produced by hens kept with roosters (such eggs are rich in steroids which commercial eggs lack); meats from animals which have not been dosed with antibiotics or hormones; foods that have not been refined and processed.

Nowadays, most foods are tampered with, and each tampering causes a loss of some vital part (or parts) rich in essential vitamins and minerals.

Whole natural foods *are* obtainable, but they are produced in comparatively small quantities and therefore are not available to the vast majority of people. This is where vitamin and mineral supplements, derived from natural sources, are so valuable. They are valuable also because

(a) They take the place of the minerals and vitamins that are destroyed during the preparation and the cooking of food. For example, vegetables lose vitamins in storage. They lose still more when peeled, cut up, and left standing in water. They lose all their vitamins when cooked, especially if soda is added, and their precious minerals and trace elements are dissolved in the cooking-water.

(b) Supplements take the place of the vitamins and minerals that are destroyed in factory-produced foods. For example, many manufactured foods are chemically bleached or coloured, emulsified, pasteurized, flavoured with synthetic substances, preserved, canned, and bottled, and all these processes destroy the vital elements in the foods. Water also is chemicalized. It has to be chlorinated to make it safe for drinking, because so much sewage and factory effluents go into our rivers nowadays. But chlorine destroys vitamin E in our foods. In some districts it is also fluoridated with sodium fluoride. This destroys vitamins *and* enzymes, one of which (phosphatase) is of vital importance to many body processes.

(c) Many people lead sedentary lives, taking little or no exercise. This reduces the production of beneficial bacteria in the bowels which manufacture vitamin B (and possibly other vitamins) for the body. Vitamin B in foods is also destroyed by chemicals which are used extensively in the food industry. Vitamin E in wheat is destroyed by chlorine-di-oxide used in breadmaking.

(*d*) Drugs such as the barbiturates (used in sleeping pills), sulpha drugs (used in the treatment of pneumonia), penicillin (used nowadays for so many things with a septic tendency), arsenic and sulpha compounds, also D.D.T., used for spraying fruit and vegetables – all these destroy vitamin B (and enzymes) in the body. Inorganic iron given for anaemia destroys vitamin E in the body. Atmospheric pollution by chimney smoke, exhaust fumes, tobacco smoke, all these destroy vitamin C in the body. Liquid paraffin, a bowel lubricant, is not absorbed by the body, but, in its passage through the body, it carries away the fat-soluble vitamins A, D, E and K which are thus lost when the paraffin is excreted.

To take vitamin and mineral supplements to make up for the vitamins and minerals that are lost and destroyed in our foods is to use the only means of self-defence we have. As one grows older the body needs even more vitamins and enzymes because more are used up by the slowing-down of body metabolism.

Specially important are vitamins B and C, because they help in the elimination of toxins from the body. For example – vitamin B will neutralize the harmful effects of drugs such as strychnine, streptomycin, and cortisone.

Specially important to older people are raw vegetable juices, vitamins A and C, and the mineral calcium, all of which help to prolong life. '*Eat a balanced diet and you will get all the vitamins and minerals you need*' is a doctor's advice. Nowadays this is quite useless, because a balanced diet with a full complement of vitamins and minerals is no longer obtainable – that is to say, the foods *are* obtainable, but most of them no longer contain the essential and vital ingredients, for the reasons already given.

Generally speaking, it is, therefore, impossible for the average person, unless he lives in the country and grows his own crops and fruit, and keeps his own hens and a cow, to get enough vitamins and minerals for his body's requirements. That is why the following natural food-supplements are advised each day:

1 halibut-liver oil capsule (for vitamin A and D)
2 or 3 bonemeal tablets (for calcium, phosphorus, and magnesium)
1 rosehip capsule (for 100 mgs of vitamin C)
1 vitamin E capsule or wheatgerm capsule
1–4 teaspoons brewer's yeast (debittered) for vitamin B
1–4 teaspoons vegetable oil (soya bean, sunflower, wheatgerm, or corn) for essential fatty acids
1–2 teaspoons crude black molasses (for iron, potassium and other minerals)
1–2 teaspoons honey (for all essential minerals, and some vitamins)
¼ cup Casilan or dried skim-milk powder (for extra protein)
¼ cup wheatgerm cereal (for extra protein, vitamins B and E and minerals)
Kelp powder, in place of table-salt (for iodine and other 'trace' elements).

*N.B. A word of warning. All the above supplements are natural foods, and are therefore safe and proper to take, because they are composed of properly-balanced constituents, in their natural setting. But beware of so-called 'vitamin' or 'multi-vitamin' pills. I know of no such pills or tablets whose constituents are combined in properly balanced proportions.*

For example a properly balanced tablet of all the B vitamins (of which there are twelve known ones) is not obtainable in Great Britain, although it may be in U.S.A.

If you look at the label on a bottle of vitamin B tablets you will notice that many of the parts that make up the B vitamin-group are missing from the tablets, and that the relative proportions of those that *are* included are all wrong – that invariably there is too much of one or too little of another.

Therefore, to take such ill-balanced preparations is not only unwise – it might be dangerous. It is even more dangerous to take 'multi-vitamin' tablets, i.e. tablets, that are supposed to contain *all* the vitamins, because to take the few vitamins they *do* contain increases your need for those they do *not* contain.

This is because all vitamins work in close co-operation with each other in the body, and, if you increase your intake of one or two of them, *you should increase your intake of all of them!*

## CHAPTER 7

## CHEMICALS IN FOOD – A MENACE TO HEALTH

In these days of food adulteration, of over-refining, processing, packeting, canning and freezing, when so many things are added to (or subtracted from) food in its natural state, it is practically impossible to get natural whole foods unless you produce your own. (If you are enterprising and have a bit of garden, you *will* produce some of them, after reading this book.)

Practically all our foods are tampered with, in one way or another.

This tampering upsets the chemical composition and balance of them. Mrs Doris Grant, in her splendid book *Housewives Beware*, published by Faber and Faber, warns housewives to beware of the chemical dragon, that, like the atom bomb, threatens to destroy us all. These harmful practices are:

(1) The spraying of growing crops (wheat, vegetables, fruit, etc.) with poisonous insecticides.
(2) The refining of wheat (extraction of the germ and bran) to make white flour, and the refining of brown sugar to make white sugar. The extraction of the germ and bran from wheat, and the refining of other cereals such as barley, and of sugar, all of which are brown in their natural state, is sheer lunacy; it robs them of their vital minerals and vitamins (more about this later).
(3) The use of artificial fertilizers in the soil on which crops are grown.
(4) The hormone injection treatment of livestock with hexoestrol, and of poultry with stilboestrol, to fatten them up and make them ready for selling sooner.

(5) The use of antibiotics in feeding-stuffs given to pigs and poultry.

(6) The use of penicillin injections into cows.

All these chemicals, sprays, and drugs become an integral part of the plant or animal tissues; then we eat the plant or animal (or its milk) and absorb from it a minute dose of the chemical or drug, and, as is well-known, the power of the infinitely small dose, given over a long period of time, is far greater than that of larger doses. (Homoeopathic treatment is based on this fact.) Continued small doses of antibiotics eaten in our meat and poultry kill the beneficial bacteria in our intestines which manufacture vitamins for us, and continued small doses of penicillin in our milk, cheese, and cream, make us insensitive to the drug if and when it ever has to be given to us in case of illness.

Of course, farmers are not supposed to sell milk from penicillin-treated cows for at least a week after treatment, but unfortunately this rule is not always obeyed, and the use of antibiotics in animal feeding-stuffs is not stopped, as it should be, a week before the animals are slaughtered.

(7) The use of chemical additives to foods (preservatives, colourings, flavourings, emulsifiers, softeners, raising agents, sweeteners, etc.) some of which are highly suspect and dangerous – for instance those used in shop bread, shop cakes, sweets, bottled and tinned juices, processed fats, jams and preserves of all kinds, soft drinks, etc.

(8) The use of synthetic materials for the making of synthetic cream, fats, meringues, and such like.

However, the chemical dragon can and will be beaten. This is what everyone should do:

1. *Wash thoroughly all shop vegetables, salads, and fruit; this will minimize the danger from poison sprays that may have been used on them. Better still, grow your*

*own vegetables and fruit. Grown on composted soil they will be so healthy that they won't need sprays or artificial fertilizers.*

2. *Avoid factory-made fats, including margarine. Use only fresh farm butter, nut butters, and cold-pressed vegetable oils such as sunflower seed oil, soya-bean oil, maize oil, etc. These are all obtainable at health food stores. A list of such shops can be obtained from The National Association of Health Food Stores, 2 Brown Street, Stockport, Lancs.*

3. *Beware of shop cakes, pastries, etc., with their synthetic cream made from synthetic fats or silicon. Meringues are sometimes made from cellulose, an ingredient of boot-polish. Make your own cakes, scones, etc., with wholewheat flour, nut butter, Barbados sugar or honey (or both).*

4. *Buy wholewheat bread – better still, buy wholewheat flour and dried yeast and make your own bread (see Chapter 8).*

5. *Use only cold-pressed vegetable oils, or beef-dripping from the joint, for all cooking and frying.*

6. *Avoid all tinned, processed, frozen, and packeted foods. Buy only fresh cream. (This contains no preservative.)*

7. *If you want first-class health you will replace meat and poultry with nuts, seeds, soya beans, farmhouse cheese and eggs, farm-bottled un-pasteurized milk, yoghourt, and dried skim-milk powder. These are all obtainable at health food stores. So, too, are pure bottled fruit and vegetable juices.*

## CHEMICALS IN WATER

In the present age, many harmful things are added to our drinking water, both intentionally and unintentionally, and it is up to each one of us to know how to antidote the long-term effect of these harmful substances. The substances which are referred to are chlorine and sodium fluoride (added intentionally) and detergents (from factory and domestic waste-pipes) agricultural residues (containing weed-killers and poison sprays), atomic wastes, and sewage, all of which find their way into our rivers and coastal waters and (via the rivers) into our water supply.

The output of these effluents and residues is increasing every year, and purified river-water is being used more and more to supplement our dwindling water-supplies from other sources. But known methods of purification cannot cope with the increasing build-up of industrial and other wastes (especially of detergents) in our river-water. The consequence is that our tap-water contains minute amounts of substances that ought not to be there (in addition to chlorine and sodium fluoride), to the great detriment of our health in the long run.

## THE DANGERS OF CHLORINE

These are explained by Mrs Grant in a document entitled *Danger from the Tap*, which she read to the London Natural Health Society in June 1962. In this historic document she explains that, because of the danger to health of sewage pollution, etc., our drinking-water has to have chemicals added to it to purify it and make it safe for drinking, but that these chemicals, added to prevent certain diseases, may be causing other diseases; that in big cities in Switzerland and France it has been found that the more 'processed' the water, the greater the incidence of cancer.

At the Seventh International Conference on Nutrition at Aachen, the committee on water issued a warning that one of the main reasons why cancer is a disease of civilization is the increasing use of water made officially drinkable by various processes.

Such water, stated the committee, is sterile and dead, and, most important of all, deprived of oxygen which plays such an important part in protecting the body against cancer. About twenty-three chemicals are used in water treatment in this country; one in particular, chlorine, is used to kill bacteria and to ensure safe drinking water. Its addition to water is regarded as one of the greatest health-measures ever introduced. So brainwashed are we that we almost regard it as good for us, yet there is much documented evidence which reveals it as far from being so harmless as most people believe and as experts assure us '*it is*'.

Some of the charges brought against chlorine are:

(*a*) It destroys enzymes and vitamins which are of supreme importance to health, especially vitamin E which is vital to the heart and arteries.

(*b*) It destroys the solvent power of water (its free carbon-dioxide) thus interfering with the work of carrying nutrients to the body cells, and of removing waste-products from the cells.

(*c*) Too much chlorine in water can lead to small amounts of lead being dissolved from the water pipes and can be an unsuspected and hidden danger to health.

Mrs Grant said that chlorination has saved millions of lives, and that its continuance is imperative until we find a safe substitute; that at Rottenburg in Holland they are experimenting with activated oxygen as a substitute for chlorine. She goes on to warn people about the dangers of drinking softened water, and also about the dangers of fluoridated water. The addition of sodium-fluoride, at one part per million, is intended as a measure to reduce dental caries in children's teeth; but there are other more accurate ways of giving it to children whose parents wish them to have it. Fluoridation of our water-supply is ethically wrong; it is enforced mass-medication, without precedent in the whole history of Medicine. It precludes the right of every individual to determine what shall be done to his own body; it is mass-medication without excuse, and takes no account of the utter impossibility of controlling the dose (so that each child gets only a so-called 'safe' dose) because some children drink a lot of water, others none at all.

Many things, including tea (also natural water in many parts of Britain) contain minute amounts of fluoride; so the British, who are such big tea-drinkers, ought not to suffer from dental caries if this is caused, as some authorities tell us it is, by a lack of fluoride in the blood.

But the truth of the matter is that lack of fluoride is *not* the cause of dental caries in children; the cause is a lack of other more important and vital elements in the child's diet, due chiefly to the eating of white bread, white-flour products, and white sugar.

If children could be induced to give up eating sweets, ice-cream, highly coloured soft drinks, and all other white-sugar products, and, instead, would munch an apple or suck an orange when thirsty; and if their mothers would provide wholewheat bread and honey for them instead of white bread and white-sugar jam, their general health would improve, and their teeth and their gums would give no trouble.

If sodium fluoride is added to natural water which already contains a minute amount of it, most people (because most people are tea drinkers) are in danger of getting an over-dose of it, and it is a poison that, over a period of years, accumulates in the body and causes dread diseases.

The only semi-effective way of removing sodium fluoride from water is by filtering it through activated charcoal, but to do this is costly; the necessary apparatus may cost as much as £200, or more.

The alternatives to filtering are:

1. *The use of distilled water for drinking; it can be bought from a chemist.*
2. *The sinking of a well. This costs £200–£300.*
3. *A move to another district where the water is not fluoridated.*

Chlorine can be removed from water by boiling.
It passes off in the steam.

## CHAPTER 8

## ABOUT BREAD, NUTS AND SEEDS

White bread, also cakes, biscuits, etc., made of white flour, is practically valueless food. White bread is made of grain that, in the milling, has been deprived of its germ and bran and, therefore, of many of its minerals and vitamins, all of which our bodies need and are unable to get from other sources.

Mrs Doris Grant, in her book *Your Bread and Your Life* (published by Faber and Faber) also strongly criticizes white flour. As she says, not only is it deficient in vital minerals and vitamins, but it is positively harmful to health, firstly because, after grinding, it is bleached with chlorine dioxide (dyox). This substance is toxic to laboratory animals and, according to Sir Robert McCarrison, the world-famous biochemist, its use should not be permitted in human foods. Secondly, white flour is harmful to health because it is 'enriched' with synthetic vitamins. These are manufactured from coal-tar and other substances. They have a drug effect and can act as slow poisons to the body.

Mrs Grant says many experts are now warning that the addition to our bread of vitamins in synthetic form may be just as harmful as the deficiencies themselves.

Much has been written on the subject of natural versus synthetic vitamins, and many experiments have been done which have shown that the latter are inferior and do not act in the same way as vitamins in natural food-substances, although their chemical structure may be the same. Synthetic vitamin D, for instance, has failed to be as effective as the natural one, and, where massive doses are given, can prove dangerous.

The difference in their action lies in the fact that naturally-occurring vitamins and minerals are all complexes, and the presence of all the other members of their complex is necessary to make them act in the right way. There is an inescapable relationship existing between them. Certain vitamins are complementary to certain other vitamins; that is why white bread is such an unbalanced food – too many important parts are missing from it, and the remaining ones are crippled and act in the wrong way.

Thirdly, white flour is harmful because chalk (creta preparata is the trade-name for it) is added, and this raises the blood-pressure and damages the heart.

Other things used in white bread are propionic acid and emulsifiers. These are used to counteract the drying effect of other chemicals used, and to give the bread a plumped-up moist appearance. They have no food value whatsoever; indeed, they are harmful in that they destroy fatty-acids in other foods. These fatty-acids are essential for health of the skin and of the gut-lining, and so harmful substances which destroy them may cause skin troubles and peptic ulcers. They are chemically similar to detergents used for washing, which are well known as a cause of skin troubles. They are used only in minute amounts, of course, but minute amounts of any substance do more harm (or good, as the case may be) than larger amounts, if taken for any length of time. The smaller the dose, the more deadly it becomes over a period of years – the power of the infinitesimally small dose being the basis of homoeopathic medicine.

All these harmful substances that are added to white flour (which has already been robbed of its vitamins and minerals) act as slow poisons.

Many people are beginning to realize the danger that lies in the cumulative effect of the chemicals with which our food is grown, sprayed, preserved, and processed in various ways, but they believe there is no alternative to harmful foods, that they may as well ignore the situation since there is nothing they can do about it.

Mrs Grant's book, *Housewives Beware* (published by Faber and Faber), has been written to tell the housewife that there *is* something she can do about it; that whole-wheat bread, by virtue of its power to improve our general health, is a powerful antidote to all the poisons with which our food gets contaminated; that alternatives *are* obtainable to processed cheese, heat-treated milk, eggs from battery hens, packet cereals, factory-made cakes (containing a poisonous chemical called polyoxyethylene), bottled fruit-juices (boosted with chemical preservatives, colouring flavourings, and gases), and to white bread and white sugar.

The alternatives are fresh farmhouse cheese, un-pasteurized *farm-bottled* milk (which costs little more than pasteurized milk); eggs from free-run hens; wholegrain un-treated cereals (i.e. untreated with poison sprays while growing); home-made cakes made of butter, eggs, brown sugar or honey, and wholewheat flour; fresh fruit juices; fruit and vegetables grown on soil fertilized with organic fertilizers; wholewheat bread, preferably made at home, containing nothing but wholewheat flour, yeast, sugar, salt and water.

If you buy your bread rather than make it at home, make sure that it is genuine wholewheat bread. Some bread which is sold as brown bread is not made with wholewheat flour but with a mixture of white flour, bran, middlings, and brown colouring-matter.

Many people buy this bread, and pay more for it than for white bread, in the belief that it is the real thing, whereas in fact it is no better than white bread. Genuine wholewheat bread is made from wholewheat flour, obtainable at health foods shops. All the other things mentioned above are also obtainable at health foods stores. Wholewheat flour has had nothing subtracted from it or added to it; neither has it been chemically treated in any way, either before or after milling. This flour, also bread made from it, is obtainable in most towns, but bakers who use it are few and far between.

There is, of course, no bread like home-made bread, and it is very simple to make, far less trouble than pastry. Here is the recipe for a large loaf.

*Put 1 lb. of wholewheat flour into a large bowl with one teaspoonful of sea-salt. Put half an ounce of yeast (fresh or dried), one teaspoonful of brown sugar, and a quarter of a pint of warm water (blood heat) into another (smaller) bowl.*

*Let it stand ten to fifteen minutes, to froth up. Then, make a well in the centre of the flour and pour the yeast-mixture into it, together with another quarter pint of warm water. Mix to a stiff dough, but kneading is not necessary.*

*Put the dough into a 2 lb. bread (or cake) tin, which has been warmed, and greased with vegetable oil (corn or almond). Leave it to rise in a warm place for about 30 minutes.*

*When it has risen to the top of the tin, pick up the tin and drop it gently on to the table. This will settle the dough, if it has over-risen.*

*Place on the top shelf in a moderate oven (Regulo 5) and bake for 40 to 45 minutes. It is cooked when, on tapping it with the knuckles, it sounds hollow.*

*Remove the tin from the oven and place on a damp dish-cloth for a few minutes; this will loosen the bread if it has stuck to the tin, and help to make it easier to turn out.*

*Before baking, place a shallow dish of water in the bottom of the oven. This will keep the crust moist and prevent it being tough.*

## NUTS AND SEEDS

These are Nature's richest storehouses; they are perfect food for humans and animals. They are rich in protein, fats, carbohydrates, vitamins B and E, and minerals.

Their protein content, combined with the protein of wholewheat grain and whole raw milk, is sufficient for all bodily needs, making the eating of meat unnecessary. Moreover, they contain the germ of life; they are alive, not dead like meat.

One of their most important constituents is lecithin,

without which the body could not function. (Lecithin is also found in egg-yolk, kidneys, soya-beans, and dairy produce.)

Sunflower seeds are particularly rich in protein (52 per cent). Pinekernels contain 31 per cent, peanuts 28 per cent. Millet seeds, sesame seeds, pumpkin seeds, cashew nuts, and hazel nuts, are all rich in protein.

According to one authority, the protein in sunflower seeds is of higher biological value than the protein in meat, eggs, or fish. It contains all the amino-acids needed for the re-building and repair of body tissues, in a form that is readily utilized, and, unlike animal protein, nut-protein does not cause intestinal putrefaction.

Sunflower seeds are rich in vitamins A, B and D; also in unsaturated fatty-acids, and in calcium, phosphorus, iron, iodine, potassium, magnesium, and other 'trace' elements.

This applies to nearly all seeds and nuts, which are also a rich source of vitamin E. The vitamin E content is highest in pecan nuts, Brazils, walnuts, almonds, and peanuts.

*Almonds and Brazil nuts are alkaline-producing foods.*
*Almonds are rich in potassium and iron.*
*Pinekernels and Brazils are rich in calcium, magnesium and copper.*
*Hazel nuts are rich in iron and phosphorus.*

Chestnuts contain more starch than anything else, and, although they are nutritious, they have a low protein, fat, and mineral content.

## CHAPTER 9

## THE SIX 'WONDER' FOODS

These are brewer's yeast, wheatgerm, millet seed, yoghourt, honey, and molasses.

Others, such as potatoes and garlic, are remedies as well as foods.

BREWER'S YEAST. This is one of the best sources of protein. It also contains all the B vitamins (except B12), as well as five other vitamins and fourteen essential minerals, including phosphorus and iron.

It contains no fats, starches, or sugars, so is not fattening. It improves digestion, gives energy, and does wonders for nerves and nervous debility.

A very good pick-me-up can be made as follows:

*Mix together (with a whisk or in an electric mixer) a quarter of a pint of fresh milk (preferably unpasteurized), one tablespoonful of skim-milk powder, one teaspoonful of honey and 1–4 teaspoonsful of brewer's yeast powder (debittered). It is best to start with one teaspoonful of the yeast and increase gradually.*

WHEATGERM. This is the most valuable part of the wheat grain. It is excluded from white flour, thereby robbing such flour of its B vitamins, also of iron and calcium. It is the richest source of vitamin E. It can be bought in sealed 1 lb packets at all health foods stores and at most chemists. Half a cupful supplies 24 grams of protein, and should be eaten daily, to supplement other protein foods.

MILLET SEED. This contains a richer store of vitamins than any other cereal. It is the only grain that can supply *all* the vitamins needed by humans. It contains also all the essential amino-acids, and its protein, therefore, is equal in value to animal protein. Moreover, unlike protein, it is not acid-forming.

YOGHOURT. Yoghourt is soured milk (cow's or goat's). It stimulates the growth of beneficial bacteria in the large intestine. These bacteria manufacture vitamin B and D; they also destroy the harmful bacteria which breed there (the result of eating flesh foods, generally).

Yoghourt is a wonderful bowel cleanser and purifier. Like milk, it is rich in protein and minerals. Its protein is partly pre-digested by bacteria-ferments during its culture, and it is, therefore, more suitable than plain milk for people with digestive troubles such as duodenal ulcer and enteritis. Its calcium is more easily absorbed by the body than the calcium in sweet milk. Like cheese, milk, and buttermilk, yoghourt requires an acid medium for its proper absorption, so, like cheese and milk, it is best eaten with proteins and acid fruits. If eaten with starches and sugars, which require an alkaline medium for their digestion, its calcium changes chemically and is not available, *as* calcium, to the body.

It is quite simple to make at home, and home-made yoghourt, made with cow's or goat's milk, costs half the price of bought yoghourt (a recipe for making it is given below). The best bought yoghourt is made of goat's milk and is obtainable from most health foods stores.

RECIPE FOR YOGHOURT

A fruit-bottling thermometer and a wide-mouthed thermos jar are necessary accessories:

*Heat 1 pint of milk (preferably unpasteurized) to 180° F. Allow to cool to 120° F. Add 1 teaspoonful of 'Culture'. (This is obtainable from Gilbert Harris, Fitzjohn's Farm, Barby Road, Rugby.) Pour into the thermos jar and allow to incubate for about 6–8 hours.*
*It thickens and is then ready for use.*

CRUDE BLACK MOLASSES is the first extraction of sugar from the sugar-cane before it is refined. It is very rich in natural sugars, in copper, manganese, potassium, calcium, and all the B group of vitamins, except B1. A most important constituent of molasses is phosphoric acid, a deficiency of which (plus potassium) causes a breakdown of body cells, especially the cells which form the brain and nerves.

Many people suffering from the following ailments have been restored to health by this natural and harmless food when all orthodox medical treatments had failed to help them. These ailments include:

1. Anaemia.
2. Tuberculosis.
3. Arthritis.
4. Gallstones.
5. Bladder troubles.
6. Constipation.
7. Colitis.
8. Varicose veins.
9. Ulcers of all kinds.
10. Growths of all kinds.
11. High blood pressure and heart troubles.

*For Gallstones.* Molasses should be combined with 3–4 teaspoonsful of oil of Harlem. (This is sulphurated oil, with refined turpentine.)

*For Bladder.* Molasses should be combined with parsley juice or parsley tea.

*For Constipation.* Molasses should be combined with linseed oil or ground linseed. (One teaspoonful of each, taken at bedtime, in hot water).

HONEY has been used as a food and as a medicine from the earliest times. The Roman formula for long life was *'Oleo externus, internus melle'*, which, being translated, means 'Use oil externally, honey internally.'

The Bible speaks of a land *'flowing with milk and honey'*.

Hippocrates, the renowned physician of the fourth century B.C., who lived to be 101, is known to have recommended it to his patients.

Democritus, the Greek scientist who lived to be 109, was a believer in a sparse diet which included honey, and Pythagoras, who was a vegetarian, is reputed to have lived almost entirely on milk and honey in his old-age.

In olden times, honey mead (a sort of beer made with honey) was drunk by newly-married couples for the first thirty days of their union in order to procure fertility, and from this custom the term 'honeymoon' is derived.

The chemical composition of honey varies with the district from which the bees take it. The pollen of some flowers has a higher vitamin C content than others. The mineral content varies, too, with the district. Heather honey, for instance, is richer than other varieties in iron and copper, as its darker colour would suggest.

Besides Vitamin C and some protein, good honey contains Vitamin A and Vitamin E, and minerals such as potassium, phosphorus, calcium, iron, copper, silica, sulphur, chlorine, manganese, and magnesium. It is the purest and richest source of natural sugars, and, for this reason, is a greater energy builder and heart tonic than any other food. Dates are a close runner-up, being very rich in natural sugars.

Honey is easily and rapidly absorbed into the system, being pre-digested, as it were, by the bees, and for this reason it is suitable for invalids and for people with weak digestions. A teaspoonful mixed with 5 drops of oil of lavender is an aid to digestion.

Honey has a powerful bactericidal action, being lethal to typhoid, enteric, dysentery, and many other harmful bacteria.

Combined with an equal part of cod-liver oil, and applied on lint to styes, boils, carbuncles, and other swellings, it is completely curative. This is due to its power to draw to the site of the swelling the body-fluids which contain anti-bodies. These anti-bodies, together with its own bactericidal power, overcome the infection.

A little warm honey, dropped into the ear, will relieve

pain and inflammation. Warm vinegar and honey, used as a gargle, is a cure for loss of voice and sore throat. Borax and honey should be used for ulcerated mouth and tongue. An irritating cough due to bronchial catarrh can be greatly relieved by frequent sips of a mixture of three parts honey, one part lemon juice, and one part glycerine.

Honey can be used as a dressing for wounds of all kinds, for burns, for ulcerations, and as an eye-wash, with warm water, for sore or inflamed eyes. (Use $\frac{1}{4}$ of a teaspoonful of honey to $\frac{1}{2}$ a pint of warm water.)

It is not usually known that barley-water, made with brown 'pot' barley, to which has been added a teaspoonful of honey, is a cure for diarrhoea, and that bran-tea, sweetened with honey, is a cure for constipation. In both cases, make $\frac{1}{2}$ a pint of the brew every day, and take frequent sips all day.

Honey is a wonderful sedative and sleep-promoter; one teaspoonful taken in a glass of hot milk or a cupful of Slippery Elm beverage will ensure sound sleep. It is a magic remedy for a weak or tired heart, for high blood-pressure, and in pneumonia, where there is always a great strain on the heart. It is antiseptic, soothes pain, hastens healing, and can be applied together with castor oil to burns and scalds. (See *Honey and Your Health* by Drs Beck and Smedley.) Honey gathered by wild bees from the tropical forests of Guatemala is uncontaminated by poison sprays. You can get it at all health foods shops.

POTATOES

A diet consisting of nothing but potatoes (cooked in their skins), potato-peel water (see page 77), toasted bread, or sips of home-made unsweetened barley-water, is a quick cure for many ailments. These include colds, bronchitis, influenza, fevers (including rheumatic fever), digestive troubles, obstinate skin diseases, and nettlerash. All these ailments are due to an excess of acid poison-waste in the system, and the following is an explanation of how the potato diet gets rid of this pent-up toxic waste:

Potatoes, and potato water, are full of alkaline minerals, and the starch of the bread, when toasted, is converted to dextrin, which has an alkaline reaction also. These particular foods stimulate a copious flow af alkaline saliva, and of gastric and intestinal juices, and with this flow of secretions comes the pent-up accumulation of toxic wastes which are the cause of the feverish or toxic condition of the body.

As these toxic wastes enter the digestive tract they are neutralized by the alkaline-forming potato and the dextrinized starch. So, by means of an increased flow of the digestive juices, the blood is relieved of its acid toxins which are the underlying cause of all the trouble. (See *Potatoes as Food and Medicine* by Dr Valentine Knaggs, pamphlet published by C. W. Daniel Co. Ltd.)

The barley-water should be included only if potato-water (which is far better) is greatly disliked. The above diet need be used only for a few days, or until good results show themselves. The daily menus can be on the following lines:

*On rising.* Drink a cupful of warmed potato-peel water or barley-water.

*Breakfast.* Can consist of toasted bread and a little unsalted butter.

*Mid-morning.* A drink of potato-water or barley-water.

*Lunch.* Baked potato in its skin. (*No salt or pepper, but a knob of butter can be added.*)

*Tea.* A cup of potato-water or barley-water.

*Supper.* Baked potato (*a knob of butter may be added*).

*On retiring.* Drink of potato-peel water, or barley water.

GARLIC contains allicin, a natural antibiotic, which is a powerful antidote to disease bacteria. It is a wonderful preventive and cure for all gastro-intestinal disorders, when, in the form of giddiness, headache, and general malaise, there is evidence of absorption of the toxic products of bowel putrefaction.

It destroys the disease-causing bacteria in the intestines through its strong antiseptic and anti-putrefaction properties. It is, therefore, the remedy 'par excellence' for both sorts of colitis (mucous and ulcerative), for acute enteritis, dysentery, and for chronic diarrhoea, even when the diarrhoea is associated with tuberculosis or with cancer.

It relieves fermentation, flatulence, and dyspepsia. It exerts a very beneficial effect upon all lung complaints, including bronchial asthma, bronchitis, bronchiectasis, emphysema, tuberculosis, etc.

It is also a very effective remedy for high blood-pressure and for hypertension in elderly people, and Dr Huss of Sweden has used it with great success in the preventive treatment of poliomyelitis. It has been proved by experiments on mice that garlic is a powerful preventive of tumour growths and of cancer.

A few doses will fight off a cold better than aspirin or so-called 'cold-cures', especially if accompanied by daily doses of vitamin C in the form of rose-hip tablets.

If you don't like the taste and smell of the natural bulb as it comes from the garden, you can take it in tablet form (garlic tablets are tasteless and odourless). The dose for intestinal complaints is two tablets three times a day – in severe cases the dose should be two tablets five times a day. (*The tablets are more easily digested than the gelatine oil-of-garlic capsules.*)

## CHAPTER 10

# THE CURATIVE POWER OF NATURAL JUICES

For imparting vitality, for helping to build up resistance to disease, and for keeping an alkaline balance of the blood – raw juices have no equal. They should form part of the daily diet of every man, woman, and child.

The millions of cells of which our bodies are composed are surrounded by, and live in, a fluid called 'intercellular' fluid, and it is known that this fluid, as well as the blood with which it is in continual interchange, should be kept slightly alkaline; if it becomes acid, it is not normal and, therefore, not healthy.

In order to keep this internal ocean alkaline, we must, therefore, eat alkaline-forming foods, the chief of which are vegetables of all kinds (including potatoes).

Vegetables are better alkalizers than fruits; they also supply more sodium, magnesium, and iron. Fruits *do* contain alkalis but they also contain free acids, especially citrus fruits (oranges, lemons, and grapefruit). When the internal ocean has become abnormal (i.e. slightly acid) it needs neutralizing with pure alkalis which only vegetables can supply.

All raw vegetable juices and fruits have wonderful healing power, because, in addition to their vitamin and mineral content, they are full of life-giving energy.

For older people, juices are doubly valuable because often the chewing of salads and vegetables is difficult. Also, if juiced, larger quantities of raw vegetables can be eaten, there is no loss of vitamins or minerals due to cooking, and the vitamins and minerals in the extracted juice are more easily absorbed by the body.

The mineral content of plants is derived from the soil

in which they are grown, and methods of agriculture, therefore, assume great importance from the point of view of diet. Wrong methods of cropping, and insufficient or harmful dressing of the soil, may lead to soil depletion, and without a healthy soil there cannot be healthy plants nor healthy people. Mineral-and-vitamin-deficient soils *can* yield only mineral-and-vitamin-deficient plants, and people eating the plants will, inevitably, also suffer from mineral and vitamin shortages. As far as possible, therefore, it is best to grow your own fruit and vegetables and salads, on rich composted soil, thus ensuring your supply of vitamins and minerals (see Chapter 15).

Losses of certain minerals and vitamins inevitably occur during transport from grower to market, and from market to shop. These losses you can avoid by buying direct from a market gardener, or by growing your own.

Soaking vegetables in water for more than five minutes also causes further loss of vital elements, to say nothing of cooking, which causes still further losses. These losses you can avoid by washing and preparing your vegetables just before you are ready to cook them (*not*, as so many people do, some hours in advance) or by juicing them in a juice-press instead of cooking them. This will conserve *all* their precious vitamins and minerals. Cooking destroys them to a very great extent.

Remember, when preparing meals, that within reasonable limits, the less preparation that goes into the making of a meal, the better that meal will be from a nutritional point of view. *Natural raw foods are better than cooked ones, and they should make up the greater part of everyone's diet.*

The only things that *must* be cooked are flesh foods, bread dough, green beans and broad beans, and eggs. (The yolk of egg *can* be eaten raw, but white of egg should never be eaten uncooked.) So, while we cannot do without it entirely, heat should be used as little as possible in the preparation of our foods because it destroys their vitamins and enzymes (digestive ferments) and thus renders them less digestible and absorbable.

CARROT JUICE. Carrots contain nearly all the vitamins and minerals required by the human body. They are very rich in calcium, iron, potassium, magnesium, manganese, sodium, silicon, and iodine. They also contain small amounts of sulphur, chlorine, and phosphorus, all of which make carrot juice a wonderful remedy for all forms of ill-health due to acidity of the system, i.e. for ulceration of the mouth, lips, gums, and stomach; and for all forms of rheumatism, gout, and arthritis.

Half a glassful, taken on an empty stomach, will quickly relieve burning, due to acidity; taken fasting, with milk (or, better still, buttermilk), it will cure constipation and colitis.

Recently, the juice has been used with great success in the treatment of cancer of the stomach or bowel, but in these cases all other food must be omitted, and carrot juice *only* taken, for thirty days.

A woman with cancer of the stomach was sent home from hospital to die, but she took 2 pints of carrot juice daily for about a month, with little or nothing else, and the result was miraculous. This is not the only case that has responded to raw juices; others have responded to fasting on grape juice only. See Dr Wright's book *Foods for Good Health and Healing*, also *Raw Food Treatment of Cancer* by Dr K. Nolfi (a pamphlet published by the Vegetarian Society, 53 Marloes Road, London W8).

In serious illness, and for fatigue due to acidity, a wine-glassful should be sipped three or four times a day.

Carrots contain large amounts of vitamin A in the form of carotene; also some vitamin B, C and G. Carrot juice is delicious either by itself or combined with other juices, such as parsley, celery, beetroot, cucumber, etc. If you have no juice-press, you can obtain it ready for use, in bottles, at health foods stores in London and other big cities. It is imported from Switzerland. Beetroot juice, celery juice, and tomato juice are also available.

POTATO JUICE is very alkaline; it is also very rich in pure protein, minus starch. (The starch part of the potato is in the pulp.) Potato juice is *the* remedy for arthritis and rheumatism. If you have no juice-press, scrub potatoes, then peel thickly, boil the peelings, and drink the water.

CABBAGE JUICE. This is a great blood alkalizer. It is reputed to be a cure for duodenal ulcers if taken while fasting over a period of two to three weeks. The addition of carrot or celery juice makes it more palatable.

SPINACH. This is rich in iron, iodine, and potassium; also vitamins A, B and E. It is very valuable in the treatment of anaemia and constipation. It tastes better if blended with other juices. *Cooked* spinach is not so valuable as raw.

PARSLEY. This is very rich in vitamins A, B, C, and E; also iron. It is better blended with other juices, as it is very potent taken by itself. Parsley tea is an excellent remedy for all bladder and kidney troubles. Dried parsley can be used for this if fresh is unobtainable.

LETTUCE. This is very rich in vitamin E. Its juice, combined with carrot juice and parsley juice, makes a very vitalizing drink.

CELERY. This is a rich source of many of the minerals and vitamins needed by the body. Its juice is very alkaline. It has, therefore, strong anti-rheumatic properties, especially if mixed with parsley and carrot juice. It aids the elimination of carbon-dioxide from the body.

CUCUMBER. This is rich in potassium, iron, magnesium, silicon, and chlorine, and contains also vitamins A, B, and C.

BEETROOT. This is one of the most valuable juices. It contains iron, calcium, potassium, chlorine, and vitamins A, B, and C. It is curative of liver and gall-bladder complaints, being a liver stimulant. It builds up red blood-cells and stimulates lymphatic activity, so is an excellent remedy for anaemia.

It is used by Dr Siegmund Schmidt of Germany, and by Dr Ferenczi of Hungary, in the treatment and prevention of leukaemia, and other forms of cancer.

DANDELION JUICE. This is rich in magnesium, potassium, sodium, chlorine, calcium, phosphorus, sulphur, silicon and iron. It also contains vitamins A, B, and C. It is used extensively for all liver troubles, and it also helps bladder and kidney difficulties. The leaves *and* flower heads should be juiced – it *can* be obtained, ready made, from good chemists.

KALE JUICE. This is very rich in vitamin A and also contains vitamins C, and B2, as well as iron, phosphorus, sulphur, and potassium.

LEMON JUICE. This is very rich in vitamin C and in bioflavonoids (substances which regulate body-chemistry and influence the life-processes).

ORANGE JUICE. This is rich in vitamin C, in fruit-sugar, and in calcium and phosphorus.

PEA-POD JUICE. This contains an insulin-like substance which is an aid to the proper functioning of the pancreas. It is indicated for diabetics.

PINEAPPLE JUICE. This is very rich in essential minerals, and in vitamins A, B, and C. It is invaluable in all throat affections, including diphtheria.

RADISH JUICE. This contains a high percentage of potassium and of sodium; also many other minerals, in addition to vitamins A, B, and C. It has a soothing and healing effect upon the mucous-membrane lining of many organs, including the stomach, the nasal sinuses, etc.

TOMATO JUICE. This is rich in many minerals including magnesium, potassium, iron, calcium, phosphorus, sodium, and iodine. It is also one of the best sources of vitamin C.

WATERCRESS. This is very rich in iron and iodine, and contains most of the vitamins and minerals. Like parsley, it should always be mixed with other juices, as, taken alone, it is too potent. It is a powerful intestinal cleanser and blood purifier.

GRAPES are rich in iron, potassium, and natural sugars, and should be eaten by everyone, especially anaemic people.

APPLE JUICE. This can be made at home. Cut the well-washed, unpeeled apples into four parts, remove the pips, and put into the juice-press. Apples are very health-giving, and everyone should eat an apple a day. It is best eaten when the stomach is empty of other food, i.e. before a meal, or at bed-time. They say 'Eat an apple going to bed makes the doctors beg their bread'.

The late Dr Bircher Benner of Zurich, whose Health Clinic is famous, explained that all fruit is more beneficial if taken at the beginning of a meal and not at the end, because the ferments in the fruit are destroyed if the fruit goes into a stomach already containing food, but that they are preserved if they go into an empty stomach.

Dyspeptics need not fear that apple juice will cause trouble; on the contrary, a sweet apple such as Cox's Orange Pippin (eaten with its peel if possible, and well chewed) will help to eliminate fermentation and heartburn in the stomach and will actually assist digestion.

Apple juice contains malic acid which is a potent germicide. It penetrates between the teeth and has a beneficial effect on septic conditions of teeth and gums. It also kills harmful bacteria in the intestines. Apples contain much pectin, and to this is ascribed their power to cure infantile diarrhoea, also colitis in adults. Dr Wright, in his book *Foods for Good Health*, describes the 'apple cures' used in colitis, dropsy, kidney-disease, gout, rheumatism, etc.

All plants (wild *and* cultivated) are more than nine-tenths water. This water can be evaporated off, leaving solids that are therefore ten times more compact (as food) than when the plant is eaten in its entirety. The following juices are obtainable in this form:

*Garlic, nettle, dandelion, horsetail, coltsfoot, wormwood, yarrow, gentian, St John's wort, birch, carrot, celery, cucumber, watercress, spinach, and rosehips.*

For remedial purposes they are to be preferred to the dried leaves and roots used in herbal medicine, and treatment with them is far superior to treatment with glandular secretions from animals, for the simple reason that animals are of a different order of life from human beings. In powdered form, Hofels Pure Foods Ltd, of Wool, Suffolk, supply the following:

*For blood Disorders*. Garlic, nettle and spinach (*1 teaspoonful with each meal*).

*For digestive Disorders*. Wormwood, yarrow and gentian (*dose as above*).

*For Heart and Nerves*. St John's wort, carrot and rose-hips.

*For Liver and Kidneys*. Dandelion, birch and celery.

*For Respiratory Organs*. Horsetail, St John's wort and coltsfoot.

*For skin Disorders*. Cucumber and watercress.

## CHAPTER 11

# MEALS BASED ON DR HAY'S SYSTEM OF DIET

Dr Hay, M.D., believed that certain classes of food are incompatible with certain other classes, if eaten together at the same meal; that, if eaten together, they cause fermentation in the stomach, and acidity of the blood.

In his book *Health via Food* published by George Harrap (now out of print, but obtainable at Free Libraries), he says many people eat perhaps the right foods in the right amounts, but fail, through ignorance of body-chemistry, to combine them in the right way, i.e. with due regard to their compatibility one with another.

This, he says is important, because, if incompatible foods are eaten together at the same meal, they do not digest well together and they cause fermentation in the stomach.

For instance, proteins (meat, fish, cheese, eggs) need an acid medium for their digestion. Starches and sugars (bread, cereals, potatoes, puddings, pastry, sweet fruits such as bananas, dates, figs, etc.) need an alkaline medium for their digestion. But the stomach cannot be both acid *and* alkaline at the same time, so, if proteins and starches are eaten together, the proteins get priority. They get an acid bath when they enter the stomach, but the starches and sugars get an acid bath too, which does not suit them at all.

Moreover (and this is even more important) they (starches and sugars) are not digested in the stomach, yet they have to wait there till the proteins are ready to move on. The result is that they start to ferment. Likewise, starches and sugars (which are to a great extent digested in the mouth by the saliva which is alkaline) should never be eaten with acid fruits, because the acid of the fruit makes the saliva acid, and it cannot then initiate the starch-and-sugar digestion.

However, sweet fruits (bananas, figs, dates, raisins, etc., which consist largely of sugar) combine with starches and may be eaten with them. Acid fruits are best eaten by themselves, as they don't really go well with other foods. Fats (butter and cream) are best eaten with starches. Milk, which contains protein and also a lot of fat, *can* be taken with other proteins, but, like cheese, it digests better by itself.

Although proteins, starches and sugars, are essential constituents of our daily diet, they are acid-producing foods and should be eaten in small quantities compared with vegetables, fruits, and salads, all of which are alkaline-producing foods.

Dr Hay advocates just two meals a day, one to be a protein meal at which no starches or sugars are eaten; the other to be a carbohydrate meal. At this meal starches and sugars can be eaten, but no *acid* fruits.

Vegetables and salads can be eaten with either meal. Acid fruits *can* precede the protein meal, but they do retard the digestion of protein, and, as I have already said, are best eaten by themselves, or with milk, for breakfast.

Nuts (except peanuts which are almost entirely protein) combine well with most things.

*The carbohydrate meal* can consist of wholewheat bread, fresh butter (unsalted for preference), cream or cottage cheese, salads, honey, etc. It can with great benefit be preceded by a half-cupful of freshly-pressed vegetable juices (carrot, cabbage, celery, lettuce, beetroot, kale, cucumber, and parsley, are richest in minerals and vitamins).

Ideally, vegetables should be gathered just before use. Green vegetables very quickly lose their vitamins when picked. The cupful of vegetable juices can be flavoured and enriched with a saltspoonful of powdered kelp (dried seaweed, rich in iodine), garlic, paprika pepper, a pinch of dried herbs (or, better still, fresh chopped herbs from the garden), the yolk of a raw egg (but not the white, which should never be eaten raw), and a little cream or milk. (The whites of eggs can be made into a baked custard, with milk, and eaten at the protein meal.)

The carbohydrate meal can be rounded off with a sweet, such as banana and cream; stewed figs and cream; steamed fig and date pudding, with sweet sauce; bread and butter pudding made with raisins or sultanas; milk pudding made with brown unpolished rice, or barley-kernels; bakewell tart; treacle tart; but not acid-fruit tarts, nor jam tarts made with acid-fruit jam. (Oranges, lemons, grapefruit, gooseberries, raspberries, plums, rhubarb, black and red currants, are all acid fruits.)

*The protein meal* can consist of meat, liver, fish, or poultry (if you are not a vegetarian), plus all vegetables (except potatoes which are starchy), cooked (without salt) in as little boiling water as possible (a few spoonfuls are enough if you keep a tight lid on the saucepan).

Do not prepare and cut up vegetables until ready to cook them. If cut up, ten minutes' cooking will be long enough for most vegetables, except perhaps root vegetables like carrots. Use the vegetable water for gravy or soup; it can be thickened with pea flour, lentil flour, or soya flour. Add half a teaspoonful of Vecon or salt-free Barmene (yeast extract), to each cupful. The vegetable water contains valuable minerals, so never throw it away. No bread, biscuits, pastry, puddings, or sweet fruit (except raisins) should be eaten at this meal; in other words, no starches or sugars.

This meal can be rounded off with cheese, or a custard made with eggs but no cornflour, or with home-made ice-cream, and a cup of dandelion coffee, sweetened (if desired) with honey, not sugar.

Vegetarians can replace meat-protein with all sorts of dishes made with nuts, millet seed, cheese, egg, soya beans, lentils, and peas. Nuts (shelled) should be stored in air-tight jars with screw tops (honey jars are ideal for this purpose), and ground at home in a small coffee mill. Ground-up nuts and seeds can be made into tasty rissoles and served with vegetables and gravy, just as meat is. Or they can be eaten raw (ground up) with half a cupful of wheatgerm cereal, half a cupful of skim-milk powder, and moistened with liquid milk. To this can be added a spoonful of brewer's yeast powder. One ounce of mixed nuts (including peanuts) is equal to 2 oz. of meat-protein. Grated cheese and eggs also provide good protein. They can be made into omelettes, or scrambled, or into cheese-soufflés and cheese pie (using soya, lentil, or pea flour instead of bread or potatoes).

As already stated, the body needs about 1¾ pints of liquid a day in the form of water or juices (or both); so, on rising in the morning, it is a good idea to drink as much boiled water (warm or cold) as you can comfortably manage. This washes out the stomach, bowels, and kidneys, and should be taken at least half an hour before breakfast. A little fresh orange or lemon juice helps the water to go down more easily.

Breakfast can consist of a cereal (wheatgerm, millet flakes, Muesli, or a mixture of all three) topped with a spoonful of honey, and creamy milk. Dried apricots or figs or raisins (preferably sun-dried) soaked in a little water overnight, can be added. They will absorb nearly all the water, but, if any remains, drink it.

This sort of breakfast has real energy value, far more than one composed of packet cereals. Wholewheat bread or toast increases the energy value, also milky coffee sweetened with Barbados sugar or honey. *Milk* is an almost complete food in itself. Although it contains only small amounts of iron, and of vitamins C and D, it contains significant amounts of every other important nutrient. Its deficiencies can be made good by orange juice (vitamin C), dried fruit, and molasses (rich in iron) and egg yolk (rich in vitamin D, provided it comes from a free-range hen).

## Chapter 12

## FASTING

Fasting, which means living on water and juices and refraining from solid food intake, has long been a religious rite. It was practised as a remedial measure thousands of years ago by ancient civilizations; then by the Greeks and Romans, and also by Christ who healed a lunatic by prayer and fasting.

Christ himself fasted for forty days, we are told, with apparently no evil consequences. No doubt He did it for spiritual reasons – to discipline Himself – but nowadays it is usually done for physical (health) reasons.

Indeed, it is thought by some authorities that modern man harms his body by not fasting occasionally, as primitive man had to do; that, by failing to use his latent physiological resources such as once supported his ancestors during periods of hunger and cold, he does not make full use of his body.

In his book *Man the Unknown*, published by Hamish Hamilton, Dr A. Karrel says that there exists in the body of man, as in all animals, biological mechanisms for the storage of food; that these were developed for meeting the cyclical changes in Nature; that it may turn out that a way of feeding the body that permits of continuous growth at a maximum rate may have unfortunate health results; that fasting may have some justification, by providing an opportunity for the operation of certain emergency mechanisms built into the body by Nature.

Also, though you may eat the best foods, it is impossible for them to nourish you properly if your system is full of wastes and poisons; these *must* be eliminated first, by fasting. For, although a food-reform diet does not add more wastes and poisons to the system, it does *not* help to draw out and eliminate wastes already deeply embedded in the system. *Only fasting will do this*. That is why fasting should usually precede diet-reform. On the other hand, diet-reform alone has cured certain sick people, but these people had free bowel evacuations every day and were suffering from some deficiency in their diet, *not* from constipation and retention of waste-products.

Most people do not understand what fasting really is and what it accomplishes: they confuse it with starving, which is something quite different.

Fasting is refraining from food when the body is in such a toxic state that food cannot be properly digested and assimilated.

Starving is going without food when the body is needing it and suffering for lack of it.

Fasting is a rational and scientific way of cleansing the body and of ridding it of disease. It is thought that it achieves this because it is based upon a natural law called 'the law of compulsory absorption'.

An explanation of this well-known law of Nature is, simply, that, when the supply of food stops, the blood is compelled to make-good the deficiency by seizing anything it can get – even waste-products. In this way, waste-products and other morbid matters that are present in the system are seized and carried away by the blood to the excretory organs, and so got rid of.

Another possible explanation of how fasting achieves detoxication of the body is the following: when no food is taken, all the millions of tiny cells of which the body is composed are given a chance of getting rid of the debris within them. They are able to throw out every bit of debris, and this is carried by the blood to the excretory organs, for expulsion from the body.

In this way, provided the bowels and the other excretory organs are working efficiently, the body is able to rid itself of all wastes and toxic substances. Of course, it can and does get rid of them, to some extent, *all* the time, but, in the majority of people, the blood and the excretory organs cannot keep pace with the rate at which these toxic substances are produced. They are the result of eating the wrong foods (or the wrong combination of foods), and of harmful mental and emotional states.

Moreover, nearly everything we eat and drink nowadays contains minute amounts of harmful substances, and the air we breathe is contaminated with foul gases, fumes, and smog. The human digestion is not equipped to deal with all these *extra* harmful substances in foods and in the air, and they have to be eliminated in addition to all the ordinary waste-products of the body. This puts a great strain on the blood and on the organs of elimination. No wonder they get overloaded and overworked! We should give them a twenty-four-hours rest from their overwork now and then – say once a week, or even once a month. This short fast would enable them to catch up on their work.

Once a year (more often if you are a meat eater) the fast should be followed by two weeks on a cleansing diet consisting solely of fresh fruits and vegetables and salads. During these two weeks, no proteins, fats, starches, or sugars, should be eaten, but plenty of water and a little milk should be drunk. The summer is the best time to choose for this period of physiological rest and cleansing, when fresh fruits and salads, etc., are plentiful, and when the diet can be combined with sun and air baths and outdoor exercise.

If the opportunity to 'clean house' is not provided by an occasional fast followed by a week (or more) on a cleansing diet, the body does its best to get rid of unwanted substances through the skin – in the form of eruptions, boils, fevers, etc. – or through the mucous-membranes of the body in the form of an excessive discharge of mucus. If it can't do this (because of lack of energy or 'life-force') more serious forms of ill-health result, such as rheumatism, arthritis, diabetes, and other chronic diseases, all of which are manifestations of auto-intoxication (self-poisoning).

The indications for fasting are as follows:

1. *Any acute or chronic condition in which there is pain, because pain poisons the gastric secretions, and so food is not only not digested but is rendered toxic to the body. The same thing occurs as a result of emotional upsets, fits of anger, etc., so do not eat when angry or upset.*
2. *Any acute or chronic condition in which there is fever, such as colds, tonsillitis, pneumonia, appendicitis, peritonitis, typhoid fever, scarlet fever, measles, acute indigestion, gastritis, enteritis, hepatitis, jaundice, colitis, cystitis, gallstones, etc. In these cases, solid food should be withheld until the trouble subsides.*

Most chronic diseases, including obesity, are helped by fasting, the one exception being advanced pulmonary tuberculosis. People with this disease should be put for two or three weeks on a near-fasting diet consisting of milk (warm from the cow), raw vegetable juices (carrot, parsley, spinach, watercress and comfrey), nettle tea, and honey.

During a fast, most people have unpleasant symptoms, but all unpleasant symptoms, such as a dirty tongue, foul breath, evil odours from bowel discharges, etc., indicate that the body was in need of a thorough cleansing and that such a cleansing is taking place; so there is nothing to worry about. There is bound to be some loss of weight too.

During the fast the body is apt to become too acid. To remedy this, the juice of a lemon should be taken, in water, once or twice a day. It can be made less bitter by adding a pinch of bicarbonate of soda to the water, which will also make it more beneficial.

During the fast, drink fresh juices of all kinds, diluted with water that has been boiled and allowed to cool. In very bad cases of gastritis where the stomach is inflamed, no water should be given by mouth. In these cases, an occasional glassful of warm water should be given via the rectum (lower bowel) in an enema.

In nausea, sips can be taken by mouth, or it can be given

via the rectum if sips make the nausea worse.

In acute appendicitis it may be necessary to give no water by mouth until the gastric inflammation has subsided, and even then it should be given only a spoonful at a time.

During a fast, healthy people can continue to do light work; this helps to avoid boredom and to keep the mind occupied. Sick people have no choice but to remain idle, unfortunately.

During fasting there is a tendency to feel chilly, so keep warm, especially the feet, and if the skin throws off wastes in the form of eruptions, don't suppress them – encourage the process by daily bathing in hot water to which a ½ lb. of common Epsom salts has been added, followed by a good rub-down with a rough towel.

During the fast, the bowels will not work normally, so they must have a daily wash-out with fairly warm water (temperature about 98° F.) to remove toxic wastes which will be reabsorbed into the blood if not removed. It is not too unpleasant if properly done, and it gives a wonderful feeling of cleanliness and relief.

The next most important thing to do during a fast is to banish all fears of evil consequences, to talk about it to other people as little as possible, because, knowing nothing about its benefits, they will probably try to put you off it, and alarm you by tales of ill effects. Above all, maintain your courage and don't be alarmed by unpleasant symptoms if they occur, and remember that the body has enough stored nourishment in its tissues and organs to keep it going for many weeks.

The question of what to eat *after* a fast is a most important one. If the fast was only a short one (one or two days) no special precautions need be taken except to eat very sparingly of the right foods for a few days. If the fast lasted a week or more, then it is best to take nothing but liquids, including sips of milk (a spoonful or two at a time) for the first day.

The second day, take one meal consisting of a baked potato in its jacket (nothing else), and later in the day a second meal consisting of a baked apple, or a ripe juicy raw apple (or pear), with drinks of juices between the meals.

The third day have toast and butter (two slices only) for one meal, a baked potato and a raw salad for another, and a third meal of fruit only, with sips of home-made barley-water with milk (warmed) in between meals. Continue the hot lemon drink before the first meal of the day, and a fresh apple-juice drink or raw apple at bedtime.

After the third day, gradually increase until the amount of food being eaten satisfies, but does not satiate. And do not forget that, unless the diet is a reformed one consisting of natural whole foods (as advised in this book), the toxins and wastes will form again and the symptoms of ill-health will return. Try to under-eat, in future, rather than over-eat; resolve to always get up from the table feeling that you could have eaten a little more, and never eat when not hungry, nor when over-tired, nor when emotionally upset or 'put-out'.

It is a pity that our mental hospitals are not directed by men and women who understand and practise natural curative methods such as fasting, for the cause of much mental illness is physical, and many insane people *are* insane because their bodies are in a thoroughly toxic state, and because their diet has been deficient in one or more of the essential body-nutrients. Right feeding and fasting would do much, not only for the inmates of our state hospitals and mental institutions, but for young people who go wrong, many of whom are enslaved by sex, simply because of the stimulating foodless foods they are given. Such foods cause toxaemia and imbalance of the glands.

Long fasts of two or three months' duration are not often necessary or advisable, except for cancer (see *The Fast-Way to Health* by Dr Harold Brown, published by Thorsons. Also *Cancer, its Dietetic Cause and Cure* by Dr Fere, published by Health for All Publishing Co.).

Long fasts should be undertaken only under strict supervision of an expert nutritionist or naturopath.

The drinking of large quantities of water during fasting is neither necessary nor advisable, unless really thirsty, or unless little or no urine is passed. During fasting, oxidation is increased; this increased oxidation results in combustion of toxins, and, if a lot of water is drunk, the fire of the combustion is, so to speak, 'damped down'.

In conclusion, I will quote Dr Hay's book *A New Health Era* (published by Harrap). He writes – '*If nothing more could be done for the sick than to let them severely alone, the death rate would decline markedly. If disease has slain its thousands, then feeding in illness has slain its tens of thousands and is a wanton waste of life.*'

Dr Hay goes on to tell of people with diabetes, skin diseases, asthma, epilepsy, etc., who have completely recovered as a result of abstinence from all food, other than juices, for a period of from seven to fourteen days.

He continues – '*Desire always points the way to need, but when desire has become so corrected and subjected to conventional restrictions and limitations, it ceases to be a correct guide. Better to fast for a time every few months (or once a year) until the habit-appetites are thoroughly broken. Then begin eating, only when hungry, of the natural foods, combining these compatibly, and note the change this makes in bodily conditions and in one's whole outlook on life.*'

He goes on to say – '*Many a case of acute illness has been given up to die and has been brought back to safety by the use of vegetable juices, with all food of every other sort excluded until recovery was well on the way, or until the patient again expressed a desire for food. Of all the insane practices to which the poor deluded invalid has submitted in the past, the most insane is feeding during illness – feeding anything at all except the simple juices that require practically no energy for digestion, and that leave behind nothing but alkalies, of which the body stands in great need. During sickness of any kind the body is exhibiting an acute acid state, for this is just what illness is. To add to this by the further intake of so much acid-*

*forming material as is represented by the ordinary invalid diet is surely pouring oil on fire; and when the ill recover under this form of mistreatment, it is in spite of it – never because of it.'*

'Eating, not wisely, but too well,' concludes Dr Hay – 'causes most of our illnesses, and the same thing perpetuates them.

'Yet it is so simple and easy to eat only when really hungry, and to refuse all food when not hungry, that it is a wonder that such a mistaken habit could ever have developed as eating when not hungry, and especially of taking "something" when the thought of all food is repugnant to you.

'The average doctor and the average hospital insist on nourishment in some form, no matter how ill the subject may be, under the impression that dire calamity will follow if meals are missed.

'Is Man more intelligent than his little brothers? The cat or the dog, when ill, lies and sleeps most of the time, refusing all food, and, when allowed to pursue its own instincts, seldom fails to recover in a short time.

'But Man, the supreme intelligence of the Earth, who looks down on the unintelligence of the little feathered creatures incapable of reasoning, feels that Nature is not to be read literally in the matter of food, and that his own intelligence is a better guide than Nature.'

## CHAPTER 13

## HOW AND WHEN TO EAT

Much has been written about *what* to eat. Now let us read something about *when* and *how* to eat.

Eating is a necessity, but it is also partly a habit – something we do regularly at certain times of the day, irrespective of whether or not we are hungry.

Where other habits are concerned, regularity is often a good thing; (for example, the habit of going to empty the bowels at a certain time each day is a good one) but where eating is concerned it is not good.

Eating should be dictated by hunger – by real hunger, not false hunger. Real hunger is an honest desire for food; false hunger comes from nervousness or from irritation of the stomach, and is easily cured by sips of water. So here are a few simple rules to follow:

*Rule 1.* Never eat unless hungry. It is better to miss a meal (or even two) than to sit down to it if there is little or no desire for it. If you miss it, you will be all the more ready for the next one. If this rule were obeyed, fasting would rarely be necessary, except during illness.

*Rule 2.* Eat slowly and chew everything thoroughly, especially starchy foods which are partly digested in the mouth (or *should* be). Thorough mastication also helps to prevent the bad habit of over-eating.

*Rule 3.* Eat nothing between meals. Drink liquids (water, juices, or soups) a short while before a meal, but drink nothing *with* meals.

*Rule 4.* Eat moderately of everything, always getting up from the table feeling you could eat a little more. Far more ill-health is caused by over-eating than by under-eating. The body can absorb and utilize *small* quantities of food far better than large quantities.

*Rule 5.* Never eat when Nature tells you not to, nor when tired or emotionally upset. When you are very tired, the muscles of your stomach can churn only very feebly, and ability to digest food ceases temporarily; so, if you eat, you run the risk of having indigestion, because the food has to remain too long in the stomach and starts to ferment. This also happens when negative emotions, such as worry, anxiety, fear, anger, ill-will, etc., possess you. It is best then to wait until you have rested or calmed down a bit, even though it means waiting a whole day.

*Rule 6.* Make meals as simple as possible; this means avoiding several different forms of the same class of food at one meal, e.g., bread, potatoes, and pudding made of cereal or flour – all these are starchy foods, and they should not all three be included in any one meal. Likewise, meat, fish, nuts, cheese, eggs and milk, are all protein foods, and to include two or more of them in any one meal is unnecessary and unwise. A combination of two or three protein foods (or two or three starch foods) in any one meal over-taxes the digestive powers and is likely to lead, sooner or later, to indigestion or fermentation in the stomach. Too great a variety leads also to over-eating.

*Rule 7.* Eat natural, whole foods, that have not been 'processed' or over-refined, that have been grown with natural 'organic' fertilizers, and that are uncontaminated by poison sprays and insecticides. This may entail growing them yourself, to a very great extent.

*Rule 8.* Banish the frying-pan from your kitchen; no matter what sort of fat is used for frying, fried foods are indigestible. Condiments, relishes, sauces, salad dressings made with vinegar, etc., should also be avoided, although spices such as cloves, cinnamon, nutmeg, bay leaves, etc. – in fact all spices – can, and should, be used; spices contain powerful anti-oxidants that protect essential fatty acids and vitamin E. Condiments and sauces can be replaced by kelp powder, celery powder, onion powder, garlic powder, paprika pepper (rich in vitamin C), soya-bean oil (or sunflower-seed oil) and cider-vinegar. A wholesome salad-dressing made of cider-vinegar and olive-oil is obtainable from health foods shops.

*Rule 9*. Meat, if eaten, should not be taken more than every other day in winter, and not more than twice a week in hot weather. If eaten oftener, it produces an abnormal amount of toxic waste material, and this builds disease of all sorts.

## CHAPTER 14

## THE CASE FOR VEGETARIANISM

*'It is impossible to challenge the statement that the human body can be adequately nourished on a vegetarian diet. Nutritional Research has established sound scientific foundation for the belief that Man can live healthily and happily without meat and other flesh foods.'*

This was stated by Sir Jack Drummond, wartime adviser to the Ministry of Food.

Then, in 1947, the Nutrition Committee of the British Medical Association made a critical analysis of Man's protein requirements, and this is what was stated in their report:

*'It is immaterial whether the essential protein units are derived from plant or from animal foods, provided they supply an appropriate mixture of the essential units in assimilable form. There is no evidence that animal protein has an intrinsic value of its own.'*

The above disposes of the usual arguments *against* vegetarianism. Let us now examine the arguments in its favour.

First, meat-eating entails the employment of men to do the killing. Such work brutalizes, destroying self-respect and all tender feelings of compassion for the innocent harmless creatures who cannot defend themselves. Meat-eating is a denial of the right of animals to live and develop in their own way; it is the antithesis of *'a reverence for life'* which Dr Albert Schweitzer considers essential to each one of us for our moral and spiritual health, upon which depends, to a very great extent, our physical health and well-being.

Meat, being a stimulant, stimulates the desire for other stimulants such as alcohol and narcotics. It encourages in Man not only physical lust but an aggressive spirit, and an aggressive spirit leads to wars.

Meat-eating leads also to world food-shortage, because flesh foods (except fish) need more land for their cultivation than non-flesh foods (crops and cereals).

A glance at the following analysis by Dr Charles Hunter shows what crop can be produced in a year on 100 acres of land, and the number of people it can support:

| Kind of crop | Pounds per 100 acres | People fed in a year |
|---|---|---|
| Mutton | 26,000 | 41 |
| Milk | 193,000 | 53 |
| Wheat | 150,000 | 250 |
| Potatoes | 1,430,000 | 683 |

It is evident that slaughter foods need more land and feed fewer people than plant foods. Also, the total acreage of available fertile land in the world is very limited and will not support meat-eating communities – that is to say, it may be able to do so in certain parts of the world, but not in other parts. This means that communities in these other parts have to live on a starvation diet because of a lack of fertile land. This results in their attempt to acquire more land, and this causes wars. So long as Man continues to be a meat-eater, therefore, wars and famine are inevitable.

Man's health, too, is adversely affected by meat-eating, because the tissues, organs, and vessels of the animal (all of which are eaten by him) contain not only its waste-products but also the drugs, serums, and vaccines with which it was dosed when alive. These are all harmful substances.

During its lifetime, an animal's bodily functions are performed (as in Man) by the circulation of its blood which carries not only desirable substances (nutrients) but also undesirable substances (waste-products, drugs, etc.). When the animal is killed, the poisons produced in its blood by terror and pain, as well as the waste-products which were on their way out of its system via its eliminative organs, remain static in the tissues, organs, and vessels, and start to stagnate; so that, when the animal is eaten, its stagnating waste-products and poisons are eaten too.

Man's blood becomes burdened with these toxic substances in addition to his own waste-products, and a heavy burden is thus thrown upon his eliminative organs, especially the kidneys and liver.

The physical, mental, and emotional consciousness of meat-eaters is far below the level of vegetarians; their perceptions and their reactions are slower than those of vegetarians. They are less happy people, because deep down in their subconsciousness they must be aware (if only dimly) that to kill for food is wrong, especially when the killing is inhumanely done.

The least meat-eaters can do is to join the Humane Slaughter of Animals Association which is doing such splendid work on behalf of 'the creatures', to save them suffering when they are killed. The address of the Association is 17 Bolton Street, London, W.1.

Meat-eaters are more subject to cancer than vegetarians; tuberculosis, too, is more prevalent among the meat-eating nations. The Hunzas, who eat practically no meat, because, with their very limited amount of land, they cannot afford the space needed for grazing cattle, are a very healthy race. The majority of them live to be 100 or more, and cancer and tuberculosis are unknown amongst them. They eat maize and millet instead of meat.

To live on a flesh-free diet reduces the risk of insanity, cancer, tuberculosis, high blood-pressure, thrombosis, heart troubles, arterio-sclerosis, etc.

To omit flesh foods from the diet is the first essential in the treatment of liver damage, which, said the late Mr Kasper Blond – eminent authority on cancer – is the cause of *much* cancer.

A further justification for vegetarianism is provided by Ruth Harrison's book *Animal Machines* (published by Vincent Stuart). The Sunday *Observer* published two full-page extracts from it in the magazine section of their paper on March 1st and March 8th, 1964. They give a very good idea of what the book is all about, but, in case some of my readers did not see the extracts, here are the main points briefly outlined.

In her book, Mrs Harrison exposes the cruelties of modern 'factory farming' methods, which treat animals as machines rather than as living sentient creatures. On these factory-farms, all humane consideration for the animals is sacrificed to bigger production, because bigger production means bigger profits for the farmer.

The methods of rearing and of slaughter are nothing short of barbarous – uncivilized is too mild a word for them. The animals are kept huddled together, with barely enough room to stand, let alone move about. They spend their short lives in artificially-lighted windowless sheds, deprived of sunlight, fresh air, exercise, and, in the case of calves – water. Their only function is to put on weight. To hasten this process they are given growth-stimulants, hormones, tranquillizers, etc., also antibiotics to suppress disease.

At ten weeks old, the chickens are taken in crates (twelve birds in a crate) to the slaughter-houses of the packing-stations, having been starved for sixteen hours before they were packed, because undigested food after slaughter would impair their 'keeping' qualities in cold-storage.

They remain in their crates, sometimes for as long as twenty-four hours, until their turn comes. Then they are taken out of the crates, suspended by their legs on a moving conveyor belt, and, flapping wildly, each has its throat cut, in full consciousness, by a slaughter-man.

This man spends his life doing this degrading job.

The Humane Slaughter Association states that some packing-stations use mechanical stunners before throat-cutting, but others do not, because the birds do not bleed properly if they are first stunned. After throat-cutting, when the birds are thrown into a tank full of boiling water, two out of every five of them are probably still alive.

Veal calves and pigs are equally cruelly reared and killed.

Because the public demands *white* veal, the veal calves are kept, tethered and confined, in semi-darkness, and fed on a mineral-deficient diet, devoid of roughage, in order to make them anaemic.

Water is withheld from them, so that, becoming desperately thirsty, they will drink gallons and gallons of the synthetic milk-substitute, which, together with growth-stimulants and hormones, is given to them to make them fat very quickly.

The food value of such calves is doubtful; so, too, is that of pigs treated similarly, and of eggs laid by battery hens fed on pellets containing a dye to make the yolks yellow. Indeed, such unnatural foods may be harmful and cause disease.

Perhaps this all-too-brief and inadequate description of factory-farming methods (as fully described in *Animal Machines*) will produce indignation in every reader, and will spur each one to take action to try to stop such cruelties.

It has been suggested that all factory-farm produce should be labelled as such, so that housewives would have the option of refusing to buy such food. Meanwhile, they can refrain from buying battery eggs, broiler chickens, veal, and pork.

*Books and pamphlets for further reading*

*Why kill for food?* by Geoffrey Rudd, The Vegetarian Society, 53 Marloes Rd, London W8.

*The Case for Vegetarianism* by Geoffrey Rudd, The Vegetarian Society, 53 Marloes Rd, London W8.

*Diet-Reform Cook Book* by Vivian Quick, Health for All Publishing Co.

## CHAPTER 15

## HEALTH AND THE SOIL

Health is linked very closely with soil fertility, for the soil contains (or should contain) all the elements of which the bodies of plants, animals, and humans are composed. If it lacks one (or more) of these vital elements, the foods grown in it and, therefore, the animals and people who eat these foods, will also lack them. The results will be sick plants, sick animals, and sick people.

The earth on which we live was originally a rich store-house of life-sustaining elements. Its rivers and glaciers wore away the rocks of the mountains and hills, and deposited them as sediment in the soil of the valleys and plains.

Now, after millions of years, its store of these life-giving elements is nearly exhausted. The soil of the earth has been impoverished, partly by heavy rainfall which has carried away its soluble and valuable minerals to the sea, partly by removal of its primeval forests, which helped to conserve the rainfall, but chiefly by Man's bad husbandry.

Man has taken more out of the soil than he has put back into it; he has practised intensive one-crop cultivation of large areas of land. Since the invention of machinery, the land has been raped by greedy agricultural-ists who have been concerned only with getting the largest possible yield out of it, sacrificing good husbandry to weight of crop, for the sake of greater profit. To these people, the fact that high yields and large-size crops are *not* synonymous with nutritional value does not matter; all that they are concerned about is making money.

The soil can, and must, be brought back to fertility. Otherwise our food will continue to become more and

more deficient in essential nutrients. This will cause more
and more ill-health and disease: Man will become more
and more dependent upon medical services, and eventually
the world will become one vast hospital (or cemetery!).

Soil fertility can be restored by:

(a) Returning to it, in the form of compost, manure,
sewage, etc., all organic waste materials that came out
of it (excluding, of course, diseased material).

(b) Green manuring. A green crop of mustard or comfrey
is grown and ploughed in.

(c) Rotation cropping.

The application of artificial fertilizers alone (i.e. without
organic materials too) upsets the chemical balance of the
soil, causing a shortage of copper and other 'trace'
elements, including iodine. A shortage of copper means
that iron, which is an essential constituent of the body's
enzymes, becomes unavailable, because it can be assimilated by the body only in the presence of copper – hence the
importance of traces of copper in the soil on which our
foods are grown.

Without copper, the iron we obtain from them would be
useless to us, and a diminution in the enzyme content of
all our body-cells would result. Such a diminution would
be accompanied by a reduction in the resistance of the
body-cells to disease, because enzymes play a fundamental
part in the body's mechanics of defence and attack.

Other 'trace' elements (cobalt, phosphorus, manganese,
magnesium, and iodine) are of equal importance to the
efficient functioning of our bodies.

For example, iodine is essential to the proper functioning of the thyroid gland which produces hormones
(chemical messengers) that play a decisive part in the
ability of the body to defend itself against microbic attack.
We see then, that the health of plants, of animals and of
humans is linked to the proper management and the proper
treatment of the soil, from which *all* nourishment is
derived.

Foodstuffs are studied by medical scientists doing research work into the causes of disease, but these people pay little attention to the study of the soil in which the foods they study are grown; this seems to me tantamount to looking for the cause of a defect in a finished product without examining the raw materials of which it is made.

Dieticians and the diets they prescribe are, therefore, of little help or value to anyone suffering from a degenerative disease, unless the soil which produced the constituents of the diet they prescribe is taken into account.

Andre Voisin says in *Soil, Grass, and Cancer* (published by Crosby Lockwood & Son), that dietetics will progress, and preventive medicine will become effective, only when it is remembered that the soil makes the food, and the food the man, and that animals and men are biochemic photos of the soil.

In 1957, the World Health Organization (W.H.O.) issued a warning that there is a definite connection between the increasing number of deaths due to degenerative diseases and the increasing use of artificial techniques in food-production and food-processing.

Yet the food-producer continues to use chemical ferti- lizers and insecticides at every stage of crop-production, aiming at a greater control over natural processes; whereas, if he aimed at a higher content of organic matter in his soil, his crops would be so healthy that they would not need chemical remedies.

Pests and diseases do not attack healthy plants, any more than they attack healthy human beings. There are more pests and diseases among farmyard animals now than ever there were in the past when Man used the age- old idea of returning to the soil everything taken out of it, including sewage.

He now puts his hand into a bag of artificial fertilizer, and scatters it over his land. But when the soil, which is an active, living, pulsating entity, is exhausted for lack of organic materials on which to feed, it is useless to feed her with crude (inorganic) chemicals – indeed, to do so will only aggravate the sickness (the exhaustion) from which she is suffering, for you cannot cure a sick soil with crude chemicals any more than you can cure a sick man with them.

Chemicals such as sulphate of ammonia, etc., are simply stimulants which act like the proverbial whip to a tired horse – it may drag the last ounce of energy out of the creature, but may kill it in the process.

Such chemicals should be used (with great discretion) only in addition to, never instead of, organic matter. The value of artificial fertilizers lies in their ability to complement, *not* replace, the nutritional variety afforded by organic matter.

Health begins in the soil, and it should, therefore, be the concern of the Ministry of Health to make-good soil deficiencies, which are the cause of so much ill-health.

Soil deficiencies could be made good by adding to the soil fresh amounts of the grit of natural rocks (from which all soils were originally formed), the amounts and the kinds differing in different places, according to local need.

This idea comes from a book called *Bread from Stones*, written in 1833 by an apothecary, Julius Hensel, who became a doctor. He maintained that there could be no full physical or mental health, nor resistance to disease, if the mineral constituents of the body were deficient.

The cost of putting Hensel's ideas into practice would cost millions of pounds, but not more than wars and preparations for wars, and it would save millions a year at present spent on National Health services.

It would ensure that the produce of the soil (our food) contained all the minerals and trace elements essential for health. It would mean that the government would become largely responsible not only for the *treatment* of disease (as it is at present) but also for its *prevention* (as, of course, it should be).

Another way in which the government should make itself responsible for the prevention of disease is by tackling the problem of sewage disposal which has become an increasingly serious one. The filthy state of our rivers and parts of our coasts is a national disgrace, and, although millions of pounds have admittedly been spent on sewage works since the war, the problem of sewage disposal is becoming worse as the population grows and continues to grow.

Municipal composting of sewage is the answer.

It is the method used in some of our go-ahead towns already (in Edinburgh, Leicester, Leatherhead, and parts of Jersey) and should be made compulsory everywhere. The cost of the necessary machinery is soon paid for by the sale of the compost to farmers, and others. Sewage utilization *must* replace sewage disposal, because much of our drinking water comes from rivers, and, although it is well doctored and treated with chemicals to make it safe, there is always just the millionth chance of infection from it. Besides, sewage can be made into such valuable food for the soil. Perhaps readers will agree with some scientists who maintain that sewage-compost should be used only on land where animal-foods are to be grown.

Let us hope that Man will soon learn that soil-health, plant-health, and human-health, are inter-dependent, for only when he *has* learnt this, and has reverted to the practice of good husbandry of the soil, will there be an improvement in his physical and spiritual health, both of which are in a sorry state at present.

## CHAPTER 16

# A SUMMING-UP

Today, despite the latest 'wonder' drugs of science and the marvels of surgery, disease is on the increase, and there is a very close connection between this increase and present-day methods of soil cultivation, of food production, and of food preservation. The aim of these methods is 'quantity' rather than 'quality', and a longer 'shelf-life' at the expense of freshness.

To say that practically everything we eat nowadays – unless it has been grown in our gardens and fields, or produced by our own livestock – has been tampered with in one way or another by chemists and food technologists is an understatement. It has not only had vital parts removed, it has had substances added to it that are valueless to the body and that may even be harmful. We have in mind such things as commercially-grown fruit and vegetables; tinned, bottled, and packeted foods; 'cured' meats and fish; processed cheese and cooking fats; refined white foods such as white flour, white sugar, white rice and barley, etc.

The fruit, vegetables, and salads, have generally been sprayed with poisonous insecticides; the tinned, bottled, processed, and packeted foods have had preservatives and probably colouring added; and the refined white foods have been bleached. These are just a few of the harmful substances used in and on our food nowadays – there are many more.

Our drinking water, too, often comes from rivers polluted with domestic and factory wastes, and has to have chlorine added to it to make it safe. Chlorine, until something better is found, is an essential safeguard, but it destroys important enzymes in the body. So, too, does sodium-fluoride, which, in addition, is a cumulative poison and possibly carcinogenic (cancer-causing).

Another danger and a menace to health is the fume-and-smoke-laden air we are forced to breathe in built-up and industrial areas, and on the road. We need laws to ensure the purity of our air, our foods, and our water, and we need dedicated men to enforce them. There are a few, but all *too* few.

If people were sufficiently concerned about their health they would demand legislation banning the use of all poisonous chemical substances other than those proved to be non-cumulative (i.e. those that the body can get rid of) and of all unnecessary additives, (such as colourings, flavourings, etc.) in foods and liquids. Those foods and drinks that do contain chemicals should bear labels detailing the chemicals contents so that only people who wish to eat or drink them need do so – other (wiser) people could buy and eat whole natural foods and drinks, which *are* obtainable, chiefly at health foods stores.

A restriction on the sale of artificial fertilizers would mean that our farmers would turn to organic methods of soil cultivation which would produce such healthy crops that insecticides would not be needed. (For further reading on the subject, see *Our Synthetic Environment* by Lewis Herber, published by Jonathan Cape).

The government should, of course, take sterner measures to *prohibit* the sale and use of all chemicals containing cumulative poisons, and to restrict the use of *all* chemicals in (and on) foods and growing crops.

Vigorous abounding health can come only from the proper cultivation of the soil. An impoverished, undernourished soil can produce only impoverished foods, lacking in nutritive value, and such foods can produce only a C.3 nation. The government should, therefore, take steps to make mineral-deficient soils rich and fertile.

In this way, the government would become largely responsible, not only for the *treatment* of disease but for its *prevention* also, as, of course, it should be. If we want to prevent disease we have got to learn to control our environment and our way of life (by environment is meant not only what surrounds our bodies but what goes inside them too). We can do this only if helped by our legislators, the government. Without their help, people are powerless. So write to your M.P. and enlist his help.

On the other hand, the ignorance, indolence, and indifference of the vast majority of people to the all-important matters of food-production methods, of food preparation, and of nutrition, is appalling. Advice about nutrition should, of course, be given to people by their doctors, but it seldom is, and lectures on these vital subjects should be given in schools (including medical-training schools) and to parents.

People also need medical therapy that is compatible with the laws of Nature, but what they get is either drugs that simply suppress the symptoms without removing the cause of the trouble, or surgery that sometimes undermines their health for life.

Doctors should give up being satisfied with drug treatment, and should learn to recognize, and to treat, mineral (and other) deficiencies in their patients.

People who have no faith in drugs have no alternative, when ill, but to seek the advice of a naturopath or homoeopathic doctor; but this entails paying a fee, and, as many of these people pay National Health insurance, they feel unwilling, or unable, to pay private fees as well.

For this reason qualified naturopaths, osteopaths, and chiropractors should be included in the National Health Service. If they were, state hospitals would then provide treatment based on nature-cure for people who preferred it to treatment on orthodox lines.

But all this is, I'm afraid, a dream of the future. For the present, we have got to put up with things as they are and make the best of them. It behoves us all, therefore, to keep as fit as possible, so that we don't need the attention of doctors or hospitals, and my advice about how to do this is as follows:

1. *Become your own baker.* Home-made wholewheat bread, made of 100 per cent wholewheat flour, grown on soil made fertile with compost and other natural fertilizers, is the body's first line of defence against the dangers of chemicalized foods and our increasingly toxic environment. Wholewheat flour can be bought from all health foods stores, and bread made of wholewheat flour needs no kneading (for recipe, see Chapter 8).

2. *Become your own greengrocer.* If you have a garden, no matter how small, do use it to grow your own vegetables and salads, if nothing else. These freshly picked as you want them, are invaluable to health.

But first make a rubbish heap (in one corner) of waste vegetable matter (grass mowings, peelings, and all kitchen wastes, and weeds). Mix with the heap a bucketful of manure or bedroom slops (healthy human urine) to help the rotting-down process. Cover each 2 ft layer of rubbish with a sprinkling of lime and garden soil. Enclose the heap with wire netting supported at each corner by an upright stake, then cover with old sacks, topped by a sheet or two of corrugated iron (to conserve the internal heat which generates).

When the heap has rotted (in summer it takes only a few weeks to rot down into sweet-smelling compost, but in winter it takes two or three months), spread it over your garden together with some dried powdered seaweed called 'Maxicrop', and on it grow your vegetables, salads, and fruits.

They will be full of all the things our bodies need (vitamins, minerals, trace elements, and enzymes), and you will know that they are free from poisonous pesticides and sprays, *and* from artificial fertilizers which upset the chemical balance of the soil.

Remember that health begins in the soil, which is the great machine that produces *all* our nourishment – that soil science is the basis of preventive medicine, the medicine of tomorrow, and that prevention of disease is the only sure cure.

3. *Become your own dairyman.* Keep a goat and some hens, if you have room for them. Otherwise, get goat's milk (Express Dairy Co. can supply this, to order) and eggs from hens that are allowed to run and roam about. Avoid battery bird's eggs – they are deficiency foods.

4. *Eat as many uncooked foods as possible.* Cooking destroys vitamins and digestive enzymes, thus making foods less valuable and more difficult to digest and absorb. Foods that are unpalatable unless cooked (e.g. flesh foods) are best omitted from the diet.

As we grow older our bodies seem to tire of producing enzymes, year in year out; so, unless we obtain them from our foods (and only raw foods contain them), we become deficient in them. Then our digestion suffers, and this affects our general health; thus, we start to go downhill, to get ailments, and to age quickly. A diet consisting largely of raw foods would prevent and cure this unnecessary and untimely ageing process.

5. *Avoid all refined foods* that have been robbed of their vital parts, such as white flour, white sugar, white rice, pearl barley, etc. Replace them with wholewheat flour, Barbados sugar, honey, brown rice, and 'pot' barley, all of which can be bought from health foods stores.

Avoid all processed, packeted, preserved, tinned, bottled, and smoked foods, all of which contain chemicals (to preserve them and give them a longer shelf life), some of which may be harmful to human cells.

Other chemical substances such as flavourings and colourings are added to foods to deceive us into thinking that, because the foods are attractive-looking and palatable, they are, therefore, nutritious. This is not necessarily so; the highly attractive-looking and highly palatable foods may be quite worthless, devitalized foods. So, beware of highly palatable foods – they are usually low in nutritive value. There *was* a time when the palatability of a food could be taken as a reliable guide to its nutritive value, but it cannot nowadays.

6. Use no aluminium cooking or storage vessels. Stain-

less steel or good-quality enamel is best for saucepans and kettles; copper is best for preserving pans.

7. Use your legs more, and public transport less. Exercise – the kind that makes you perspire – is absolutely vital to good health, so take outdoor exercise every day, combining it with deep rhythmical breathing. Walking is splendid exercise if you know *how* to walk. When you walk you should swing the arms loosely and stride along at a good pace, not stroll, breathing in through the nose to, say, four paces, and out through the mouth to five paces. Without exercise, the blood is not properly oxygenated; also the body does not produce its own enzymes and vitamins, nor its own anti-bodies (its army of soldiers that fight disease).

8. Give up the laxative-taking habit. If your bowels do not empty themselves during the day, use a warm water 'gravity' douche before going to bed. A pint of plain warm water, held in the bowel for a few minutes, will clear away all waste matter that will poison the system if unremoved. But proper food, properly masticated, a cup of home-made bran-tea with honey, some raw vegetable juices, and regular daily exercise in the fresh air, with deep breathing, all these will, in time, if taken regularly, ensure regular bowel evacuations and a clean blood-stream.

9. Give up the cocktail habit, the tea-and-coffee-drinking habit, and the cigarette-smoking habit. Cocktails do untold harm to the kidneys and the stomach. Instead, drink apple juice, bran-tea, yarrow (and other) herb teas, and dandelion coffee. If ordinary tea is taken, it should not be taken strong, nor allowed to infuse for more than three minutes.

10. Become your own doctor. *Given the right conditions,* the human body is a self-curing mechanism. It possesses innate, instinctive intelligence, and knows how to cure itself better than any doctor knows.

The famous doctor, Sir William Osler, once said '*What Nature cannot cure must for ever remain uncured.*' Remember, only the body heals – but Man can help or retard the natural healing power of the body. He can help it by rest (including rest from solid food) supplemented by natural juices.

Become, thus, a self-sufficient, self-supporting, *'do-it-yourself'* person. Learn to depend upon yourself and not upon other people, and make yourself independent (except, of course, in the case of accidents, of doctors and hospitals.

By putting this advice into practice you will be learning to do something far more important than exploring outer space, or building bigger and better bombs, or flying to the moon.

You will be learning how to live healthfully and happily on *this* planet, the good Earth, and, in so doing, will be fulfilling God's purpose.

# THE USE OF FOOD TABLES

The nutrients in crops grown for food vary widely in quantity and quality, depending upon:

(a) The amount of sun and rain they received while growing.
(b) The degree of ripeness or maturity when harvested.
(c) The method of fertilizing the soil in which they are grown.
(d) The humus content of the soil (humus or compost feeds the bacteria and fungi, which feed the plant).
(e) The mineral content of the top soil and subsoil. Carrots, for example, have been analysed which contain no vitamin A (carotene) whatsoever. The protein content of wheat can vary from 5 to 20 per cent, depending upon the humus content of the soil in which it is grown. The nutritive value of milk, eggs, meat, etc., varies according to what the diet and the living conditions of the animals that produced them have been.

Therefore, the following food tables can be used only as a general guide in planning a diet – not an exact one.

N.B. Grms = Grams
     Mgs = Milligrams
     I.U. = International Units.

## THE MAIN MINERAL AND PROTEIN CONTENT OF EVERYDAY FOODS, IN 100 GRAMS OF EACH FOOD

| Food | Calcium mgs. | Phosphorus mgs. | Iron mgs. | Protein grams |
|---|---|---|---|---|
| Almonds | 234 | 505 | 4.7 | 20 |
| Apple (raw) | 6 | 10 | 0.3 | — |
| Apricots (raw) | 17 | 23 | 0.5 | 1 |
| Apricots (dried) | 67 | 100 | 5.5 | 5 |
| Banana (raw) | 8 | 26 | 0.7 | 1 |
| Broad beans (cooked) | 50 | 148 | 2 | 7 |
| Haricot beans (cooked) | 50 | 148 | 2 | 7 |
| Beef | 34 | 290 | 2 | 14–28 |
| Beet | 14 | 23 | 0.05 | 1 |
| Brazil nuts | 186 | 693 | 3 | 14 |
| Broccoli | 88 | 62 | 1 | 3 |
| Brussels sprouts | 32 | 72 | 1 | 4 |
| Buckwheat flour | 33 | 346 | 2 | 11 |
| Butter | 20 | 16 | — | 0.5 |
| Cabbage (raw) | 49 | 29 | 0.5 | 2 |
| Cabbage (cooked) | 44 | 20 | — | 1 |
| Carrots (raw) | 37 | 36 | 0.5 | 1 |
| Carrots (cooked) | 33 | 31 | 0.5 | 0.5 |
| Cashew nuts | 38 | 373 | 3.5 | 17 |
| Cauliflower | 21 | 42 | 0.5 | 2 |
| Celery | 39 | 28 | 0.5 | 1 |
| Cheese (Cheddar) | 750 | 478 | 1 | 28 |
| Chick peas | 75 | 150 | 6 | 50 |
| Chicken (roasted) | 11 | 265 | 1 | 28 |
| Cocoa | 133 | 648 | 10 | 16 |
| Coconut (dried) | 26 | 187 | 3 | 7 |
| Cod (broiled) | 31 | 274 | 1 | 28 |
| Cream | 102 | 80 | — | 3 |
| Cucumber (unpeeled) | 25 | 27 | 1 | 1 |
| Dates | 59 | 63 | 3 | 2 |
| Egg (cooked) | 55 | 203 | 2 | 6 |
| Egg yolk (raw) | 141 | 565 | 5.5 | 8 |
| Figs (dried) | 126 | 77 | 3 | 1 |
| Flour (wholewheat) | 41 | 372 | 3 | 13 |
| Gooseberries (cooked) | 12 | 10 | — | — |
| Grapefruit (raw) | 15 | 15 | — | — |
| Grapes | 11 | 12 | — | — |

| Food | Calcium mgs. | Phosphorus mgs. | Iron mgs. | Protein grams |
|---|---|---|---|---|
| Herrings .. .. .. | 147 | 297 | 1 | 19 |
| Honeydew melon .. .. | 14 | 16 | — | — |
| Honey (light coloured) .. | 2–8 | 2–6 | 0.25 | — |
| Honey (dark) .. .. | 1–28 | 3–7 | 2 | — |
| Kale (cooked) .. .. | 134 | 146 | 1 | 3 |
| Kidneys .. .. .. | 18 | 244 | 13 | 24 |
| Lamb (roasted) .. .. | 11 | 208 | 1 | 25 |
| Lentils .. .. .. | 25 | 119 | 2 | 9 |
| Lettuce .. .. .. | 25 | 36 | 2 | 1 |
| Liver .. .. .. | 13 | 547 | 14 | 24 |
| Milk (cow's) .. .. | 100 | 92 | — | 18 |
| Milk (dried skim) .. .. | 909 | 708 | 0.5 | 28 |
| Millet .. .. .. | 650 | 500 | 10 | 12 |
| Molasses .. .. .. | 290 | 690 | 6 | — |
| Oatmeal .. .. .. | 42 | 320 | 3 | 12 |
| Onions .. .. .. | 24 | 29 | 0.5 | 1 |
| Orange (raw) .. .. | 42 | 22 | 0.5 | 1 |
| Parsley (1 oz.) .. .. | 203 | 63 | 6 | 1 |
| Parsnip (2 oz.) .. .. | 45 | 62 | 6 | 1 |
| Peaches (dried) .. .. | 48 | 117 | 6 | — |
| Peanuts .. .. .. | 69 | 401 | 2 | 32 |
| Pears (dried) .. .. | 35 | 48 | 1 | — |
| Peas (cooked) .. .. | 56 | 76 | 0.5 | 3 |
| Peas (split) .. .. | 11 | 89 | 1 | 12 |
| Pecan nuts .. .. | 73 | 289 | 2 | 9 |
| Pistachio nuts .. .. | 139 | 500 | 7 | 19 |
| Potatoes .. .. .. | 7 | 53 | 0.5 | 2 |
| Prunes .. .. .. | 24 | 37 | 1 | 1 |
| Pumpkin seeds .. .. | 51 | 1144 | 11 | 29 |
| Radishes .. .. .. | 30 | 31 | 1 | 1 |
| Raisins .. .. .. | 62 | 101 | 3 | 2 |
| Rice (brown) .. .. | 12 | 73 | 0.5 | 2.5 |
| Rye flour .. .. .. | 38 | 376 | 3 | 12 |
| Sardines .. .. .. | 437 | 499 | 2.5 | 24 |
| Sesame seeds .. .. | 1160 | 616 | 10 | 18 |
| Soya beans .. .. .. | 67 | 114 | 3 | 40 |
| Soya flour .. .. .. | 67 | 114 | 3 | 40 |
| Spinach .. .. .. | 93 | 38 | 2 | 3 |
| Strawberries .. .. | 21 | 21 | 1 | 0.5 |

| Food | | | Calcium mgs. | Phosphorus mgs. | Iron mgs. | Protein grams |
|---|---|---|---|---|---|---|
| Sunflower seeds | .. | .. | 120 | 857 | 7 | 25 |
| Sweetbreads | .. | .. | — | 364 | 7 | 12 |
| Tomatoes (raw) | .. | .. | 13 | 27 | 0.5 | 1 |
| Turnips (tops) | .. | .. | 184 | 37 | 1 | 2 |
| Walnuts (English) | .. | .. | 99 | 380 | 1 | 21 |
| Wheatgerm | .. | .. | 72 | 1118 | 9 | 26 |
| Yeast (brewer's) powder | | .. | 70–760 | 1753 | 17 | 38 |

### VITAMIN A CONTENT OF EVERYDAY FOODS
#### (Measured in international units)

| Animal foods | per 3½ oz. | Vegetable foods | per 3½ oz. |
|---|---|---|---|
| Halibut liver oil | .. 850,000 | Carrots .. | .. 10,500 |
| Cod liver oil | .. 21,000 | Spinach .. | .. 8,100 |
| Ox liver .. | .. 5,670 | Dried apricots | .. 2,700 |
| Butter .. | .. 2,300 | Tomato .. | .. 900 |
| Margarine.. | .. 2,200 | Dried prunes | .. 750 |
| Cheese .. | .. 1,300 | Green peas | .. 610 |
| Kidney .. | .. 1,100 | Cabbage .. | .. 130 |
| Egg .. | .. 1,000 | | |
| Sardines .. | .. 270 | | |
| Milk .. | .. 70–140 | | |
| Herring .. | .. 40 | | |

*The body requires about 5,000 i.u. per day of*
*Vitamin A. 1 halibut liver oil capsule contains*
*5,000 i.u. of Vitamin A, plus 500 i.u. of Vitamin D.*

## VITAMIN B CONTENT OF EVERYDAY FOODS
### (measured in milligrams)

| Vitamin B1 | per 3½ oz. | | Vitamin B2 | | per 3½ oz. |
|---|---|---|---|---|---|
| Dried brewer's yeast | 15 | | Dried brewer's yeast | .. | 4 |
| Wholewheat bread | 1 | | Liver .. | .. | 4 |
| Potato .. | .. A trace | | Cheese .. | .. | A trace |
| Milk .. | .. — | | Egg .. | .. | A trace |
| | | | Milk .. | .. | 0.4 |

| Vitamin B3 | per 3½ oz. |
|---|---|
| Dried brewer's yeast | .. 37 |
| Liver .. | .. 16 |
| Sardines .. | .. 5 |
| Wholewheat bread | 4 |
| Potato .. | .. 1 |
| White bread | .. 0.5 |

1 oz. dried brewer's yeast = 1 tablespoonful.

*The body requires 1 mg. Vitamin B1 per day.*
*„ „ „ 1–2 mgs. Vitamin B2 per day.*
*„ „ „ 10–15 mgs. Vitamin B3 per day.*

### VITAMIN C CONTENT OF CERTAIN FOODS
#### (measured in milligrams)

|  | mgs. in 100 gms. (3½ oz.) |
|---|---:|
| Juice of 1 large orange .. .. .. .. | 60 |
| Rose hips (dried and powdered) (1 teaspoonful) | 600 |
| Blackcurrant juice (2 tablespoonsful) .. .. | 200 |
| Brussels sprouts .. .. .. .. .. | 100 |
| Cauliflower .. .. .. .. .. | 70 |
| Cabbage .. .. .. .. .. .. | 70 |
| Spinach .. .. .. .. .. .. | 65 |
| Watercress .. .. .. .. .. | 60 |
| Strawberries .. .. .. .. .. | 60 |
| Lemon juice (4 tablespoonsful).. .. | 25 |
| Grapefruit (half) .. .. .. .. .. | 40 |
| Fresh green peas .. .. .. .. | 30 |
| Tomato (one medium) .. .. .. .. | 25 |
| Potatoes, new .. .. .. .. .. | 32 |
| Oct./Nov. .. .. .. .. | 21 |
| Dec. .. .. .. .. .. | 14 |
| Jan./Feb. .. .. .. .. | 10 |
| March on .. .. .. .. | 7 |
| Apples (Bramleys) .. .. .. .. | 18 |
| Lettuce .. .. .. .. .. .. | 15 |
| Bananas (peeled).. .. .. .. .. | 10 |
| Beetroot .. .. .. .. .. .. | 10 |
| Onions .. .. .. .. .. .. | 10 |
| Carrots .. .. .. .. .. | 10 |
| Apples (Blenheim) .. .. .. .. | 4 |
| Plums .. .. .. .. .. .. | 4 |
| Pears .. .. .. .. .. .. | 4 |
| Cows' Milk (Fresh) (about ½ pint) .. .. | 2 |
| Walnuts (shelled).. .. .. .. .. | 1,800 |

*South African oranges are richer in Vitamin C. Potatoes vary according to how long they remain in storage.*

The longer they remain the more vitamin C they lose. As much as 75 per cent of the vitamin C in green vegetables may be lost in cooking.

They should be plunged into boiling water (as little as possible to cover them), cooked rapidly in a covered vessel without salt or soda, and served and eaten as soon as cooked ; they will then lose only two-thirds of their vitamin C, e.g. sprouts, starting with 100 mgs. per 100 grams when raw, will finish with 33 mgs. when cooked, but if kept hot before being eaten they will lose still more.

Seeds, grains, and dried peas and beans contain no vitamin C. When seeds have sprouted, however, vitamin C is produced, also vitamin E. If no other source of vitamin C is available, *sprouted wheat grain is a valuable source*.

Simply rinse the grain (every day) and keep it moist for two or three days until it sprouts; then eat one teaspoonful of it a day.

### VITAMIN D CONTENT OF CERTAIN FOODS
#### (*Measured in international units*)

| Dairy foods | i.u. per 3½ oz. |
|---|---|
| Butter | 60 |
| Cheese | 15 |
| Egg | 60 |

| Fish | i.u. per 3½ oz. |
|---|---|
| Cod- and halibut-liver oil | 20,000 |
| Herrings (fresh) | 850 |
| Herrings (canned) | 170 |
| Mackerel | 700 |
| Salmon (canned) | 600 |
| Sardines | 1,000 |

*Daily requirements 500 i.u.*

VITAMIN E CONTENT OF CERTAIN FOODS
(*measured in mgs.*)

|  | Milligrams |
|---|---|
| Wheatgerm oil (1 teaspoonful) .. .. .. .. | 15 |
| Soya bean oil (1 teaspoonful) .. .. .. | 15 |
| Wheatgerm (1 cupful) .. .. .. .. | 18 |
| Wholewheat bread (4 slices) .. .. .. | 2 |
| Vitamin E capsule (1) .. .. .. .. | 75 |

*Daily requirement thought to be 75–100 mgs.*

## BREATHING EXERCISE

Inhale slowly through the nose, at the same time noticing that the abdomen protrudes slightly. When the lungs feel comfortably full (but not over-full) draw in the abdomen slightly and hold the breath for a second. Then exhale slowly through the mouth on the sustained note of OO. Exhale to the utmost limit but without strain.

Alternatively, instead of exhaling on one long note, you can exhale on the notes of a scale. The breathing exercise should be practised for three minutes three times a day in the sitting or lying position.

Later it should be practised for five to ten minutes three times a day in lying, sitting, and standing position.

It is of the greatest possible benefit to digestion, to all respiratory troubles, to the heart, to bowel movements, and to the liver.

If done persistently and regularly, it will normalize high blood-pressure, and is at times of benefit to sufferers of all forms of heart trouble and diabetes.

If you are healthy, it will help to keep you so.

## PLANT AND HERBAL REMEDIES

*Apple tea.* Wash two or three cooking apples and cut them up without removing the skin or the core. Put into a jug (omitting the seeds), cover with 1½ pints of cold water (previously boiled), cover with a saucer, and stand the jug in a pan of boiling water for two hours. Strain through coarse muslin or a nylon strainer; add a little honey if desired. Apple tea can be made with the peel and cores which are usually thrown away when preparing apples for stewing. Apple tea is an excellent nerve sedative. It is also good for gout, kidney diseases, rheumatic troubles, high blood-pressure, acidity, liver, bowels, and skin infections.

The peel is particularly rich in vitamin C. It can be dried in the shade and stored in a jar for future use.

*Almond water.* (For coughs, colds, bronchitis, asthma, shortness of breath, feverish conditions.) Mix 2 oz. of ground sweet almonds to a paste with cold water. Add slowly a pint of boiling water, stirring all the time. Allow to stand (covered) for an hour, then serve.

*Barley water.* Wash two tablespoonsful of pot barley in hot water, then put it into a covered saucepan with two pints of cold water and bring it slowly to the boil. Simmer gently for two hours. Strain, add a little honey to sweeten. It is a wonderful remedy for all kidney and bladder complaints, as well as for all internal inflammatory conditions.

*Bran tea.* Into a pint of boiling water scatter a teacupful of 'washed bran'. An alternative is to use half bran and half oatmeal (coarse). Both are obtainable from most health food stores. Simmer in a covered saucepan for 40 minutes but never allow it to come up to the boil. Strain, and add honey to taste. It is a wonderful remedy for constipation, and anaemia, and, as it promotes sweating, it is a valuable remedy for coughs, colds, and sore throats.

*Camomile tea* (made in a tea-pot). Over a $\frac{1}{2}$ oz. of camomile flowers pour a pint of boiling water and allow to infuse for ten or fifteen minutes in a warm place after stirring well. Take half a teacupful half an hour before meals, three times a day, for lack of appetite, nerves, flatulence, indigestion, nervous indigestion, and general tiredness. A piece of flannel or linen soaked in a hot infusion of camomile and poppyheads will soothe a swollen face due to toothache, neuralgia, or earache. Camomile tea (hot) is also helpful to women if there is suppression of the monthly menstrual flow.

A little ground ginger and a trickle of honey can, with benefit, be added to the tea when it is taken for lack of appetite or distaste for food.

A cup of camomile tea sweetened with honey is far more reviving to tired people than a cup of ordinary tea.

Camomile tea, sponged over the exposed parts of the body, will keep away insect pests that bite and sting.

*Comfrey tea.* (For gastric ulcer, asthma, anaemia, skin troubles, etc.) This is prepared in exactly the same way as ordinary tea, in a tea-pot, using 1 oz. (2 tablespoonsful) of comfrey leaves to 1 pint of boiling water. It can be flavoured with lemon juice and sweetened with honey, or drunk like ordinary tea with milk.

For lung troubles and coughs, boil an ounce of the powdered *root* of comfrey in a pint of water for 30 minutes. Then add half a pint of new milk to the contents of the pan and warm up but do not allow to boil. Drink frequently during the day, especially when the cough is troublesome. If only half a pint of water is used, a jelly will result.

*Powdered comfrey root,* mixed to a stiff paste with water, is applied to bleedings, varicose ulcers, festering wounds, fractures, rodent ulcer, burns and scalds. It is also an excellent beauty cream. The powdered root can also be sprinkled on to cereals or porridge or soups. Taken internally, it enhances the benefit of the external applications. Comfrey contains vitamin B12 and is a wonderful blood-cleanser.

*Dandelion tea and coffee.* This can be bought ready-made from any health food store. The tea is made from the leaves, and stalks, and the coffee from the roots. The tea is used in digestive and sluggish liver disorders, constipation, kidney and bladder troubles and dropsy. The coffee (known as taraxacum coffee) will stimulate and help digestion and the kidneys. It is far superior to ordinary coffee in every way.

*Elderflower tea.* This can be made with fresh flowers

straight from the tree (when in bloom) or from dried flowers, obtainable from any herbalists. Put about an ounce of the flowers into a jug and cover with about a pint of water. Bring to the boil and simmer for 30–40 minutes in a closed pan. Strain. In another pan, infuse (but do not boil) half an ounce of mint (fresh or dried) in half a pint of water for 30 minutes. Strain. Add this liquor to the other. Sweeten with a little honey if liked. It is used for soothing the nerves, nervous headaches, colds, influenza, fevers of all kinds, for promoting sweating in pneumonia, appendicitis, and inflammatory conditions of vital organs. A compress wrung out of the hot liquor can be applied to the painful area. It is also a wonderful cosmetic and healer of small wounds and cuts.

*Elderberry conserve.* The ripe berries are black, and, mixed with crab-apples and blackberries (or by themselves), make an excellent jelly. Take equal quantities of each, stew gently for an hour or so, to extract all the juice, then strain, and to each pint of the juice add a pound of Barbados sugar. Return to the pan and bring to the boil. Allow to boil quickly for about five or ten minutes, till it 'jells' when tested on a cold plate. The conserve is an excellent remedy for sore throats and chest colds.

*Elderberry ointment.* This is made with the berries while they are still green before they ripen and become black. It is made as follows: half fill a large stone jar with berries (well washed). Cover them with camphorated oil, then cover the jar with a saucer and place in a pan of boiling water or in a very slow oven for four or five hours (the water in the pan should be kept boiling gently all the time if that method is used). Then strain through muslin, squeezing it well to extract all the juice. Put into clean bottles, for use as required. This ointment is an excellent remedy rubbed into the chest and between the shoulders for coughs, colds, bronchitis and all chest complaints. It is also a good dressing for burns, sprains, and strains.

*Elderberry tea.* This is made with dried ripe berries. Gather them when they are quite black; hang them up in

bunches in a warm kitchen or other warm place to dry
for a few days. When they are quite dry, strip the berries
from the stalks and store them in tins. They can be used for
making a tea which, taken hot, will ward off a cold and
promote perspiration. This tea will also relieve and help
painful or suppressed menstruation. The dried berries can
be used as a substitute for currants and other dried fruit
in cakes.

*Four oils* (for external use on strains, sprains, pain of
rheumatism, stiffness of joints, etc.).

Oil of cloves, oil of turpentine, camphorated oil, and
olive oil – equal quantities of each, mixed together, and
applied warmed.

*Hop tea* (for insomnia, debility, flagging appetite, and
as a nerve sedative).

Make in a pot, like ordinary tea, using $\frac{1}{2}$ oz. of dried
hops to half a pint of boiling water. Stir well and allow
to stand till cold; then strain. Warm up in a pan, and
drink, with honey added if too bitter.

*Lemon Whey.* For colds, and feverish states.

Heat a cupful of milk; when very hot, add the
juice of a lemon. This will cause curdling. After straining,
the whey is sweetened with honey and drunk as hot as
possible. A pinch of cinnamon improves its medicinal
effects.

*Linseed tea.* For colds, coughs, whooping cough, bronchitis, asthma, constipation, and for making childbirth
easier.

Into a saucepan put $1\frac{1}{2}$ pints of cold water and 2 table-
spoonfuls of linseed, 1 oz. of liquorice, and a piece of whole
ginger (if ginger is not liked this can be omitted). Simmer
gently for 30 minutes or so. Have ready in a jug 1 oz. of
clover flowers, 1 oz. of wild thyme and a sliced lemon.
Pour the boiling contents of the saucepan into the jug, add
a tablespoonful of honey, stir well; when cold, strain. Take
a few sips whenever the cough is troublesome.

*Linseed poultice* for all inflammatory conditions, especially those of the chest and lungs; pneumonia, pleurisy,

etc. (for bedsores and varicose ulcers add 1 tablespoonful charcoal powder to the linseed). In a warmed basin mix 2 tablespoonsful of linseed (or more for a bigger poultice) with a little boiling water. Stir till the mixture leaves the sides of the basin clean. Turn it out on to one half of a piece of clean lint and fold the other half over it. Apply as hot as can be tolerated.

*Marshmallow poultice*, for obstinate inflammatory and gangrenous conditions. To the crushed root add ½ an ounce of slippery elm powder. Mix to a stiff paste with a little boiling water. Spread on to lint and apply as hot as can be comfortably borne. Cover with oiled silk, cotton wool, and a bandage. Remove when dry, and repoultice with fresh paste.

*Raspberry leaf tea* for women's period pains due to suppression; also for easier labour in childbirth start taking it regularly every day from the third or fourth month of pregnancy. Use the dried leaves (from a herbalist), when fresh are not available, and make just like ordinary tea in a tea-pot, allowing it to stand for about 10 minutes under a tea-cosy, to infuse.

*Red clover* (or purple) has been used to relieve pains of cancer, but only on the advice of a fully competent practitioner. Either the freshly gathered or the dried flowers are used. Put a good handful of the flowers into a teapot (warmed) and onto them pour about a pint of boiling water. Cover the pot with a tea-cosy and allow to stand till cold. Then sieve, and warm up the liquid, drinking some of it, and using some of it for bathing the painful part or for applying as a hot fomentation to that part.

*Red clover poultice*. Directions for making this are as follows:

Take a large saucepan (brass or stainless steel). Into it pack as many clover heads as possible. Cover with cold water, put on the saucepan lid, bring contents of pan to the boil and boil for one hour. Then strain, pressing all liquor out of the clover. In this liquor boil another lot of clover heads for the same length of time. Strain off, as before, then simmer the liquor obtained from the two boilings over a low flame until it is the consistency of tar. It is then ready to use as a poultice.

*Sage tea* for anaemia and general debility, for ulcerated throat or gums, for hoarseness or loss of voice.

Make an infusion of sage in a tea-pot, using 1 oz. to a pint of boiling water. Allow to stand till cold, then sieve, and take a tablespoonful of the liquid three or four times a day. For throat and voice affections it can be used as a gargle and then swallowed. It heals and relieves sore throats, and clears a voice that has been over-strained (such as actors and clergymen get). Used with vinegar it also soothes toothache, and is an exellent hair tonic and colour-restorative (make the infusion of double strength for this).

*Thyme tea* is a standard remedy for all chest troubles. Lemon thyme is the sort used for debility. Wild thyme is the sort used for throat troubles, such as tonsillitis, relaxed throat and swollen uvula. Both sorts can be bought (dried) from a herbalist if neither grow in your garden. Wild thyme (or lemon thyme) is used together with linseed for making a very soothing and valuable remedy for any cough, including bronchitis, and whooping cough (see *Linseed tea*). It is also a valuable remedy, together with grated carrot, for children with tapeworm. An infusion of lemon thyme (made with *cold* water and allowed to stand for several hours) is one of the best remedies for nervous exhaustion and strain. Medicinally both sorts have the same effect, but in its action wild thyme is stronger than lemon thyme. It grows on the chalk South downs, and is eaten by the sheep there – hence the delicate flavour of Southdown mutton.

*Violet leaf tea* used for the relief of pain of cancerous growths especially of the throat and tongue. Put a good handful of the leaves into an earthenware jug; pour over them a pint of cold (boiled) water and leave to steep for twenty-four hours. Sieve, and take a wineglassful four times a day. Make a poultice of freshly gathered leaves, steeped in boiling water; apply this to the painful part.

*Violet flowers* are used for making a syrup which is

a valuable remedy for tuberculosis and for constipation in children. It can be bought, I believe, at certain chemists, or herbalists. To make it at home, put 4 oz. of freshly-picked violet flowers into an earthenware jug and over them pour $\frac{1}{2}$ a pint of boiling water. Cover the jug and leave to infuse for twenty-four hours. Then strain through muslin, add $\frac{1}{2}$lb. of honey to the liquid and bring almost (but not quite) to the boil. Allow to cool, then add an equal quantity of almond oil. It will soothe and heal a hacking cough. The flowers may be eaten in salads. They have a soothing effect on the nerves, and ease headaches due to lack of sleep. For this, the flower tea should be taken without the oil added.

(See also *Herbal Remedies and Recipes*, by Mary Thorne-Quelch, published by Faber and Faber.)